SHANE CARLEY

RED CUP NATION

100 PARTY DRINK RECIPES

CIDER MILL
PRESS

BOOK
PUBLISHERS

KENNEBUNKPORT, MAINE

13-Digit ISBN: 9781604336405

10-Digit ISBN: 1604336404

This book may be ordered by mail from the publisher. Please include $5.95 for postage and handling. Please support your local bookseller first!

Books published by Cider Mill Press Book Publishers are available at special discounts for bulk purchases in the United States by corporations, institutions, and other organizations. For more information, please contact the publisher.

Cider Mill Press Book Publishers
"Where good books are ready for press"
PO Box 454
12 Spring Street
Kennebunkport, Maine 04046

Visit us on the Web! www.cidermillpress.com

Cover and interior design by Jon Chaiet

Typography: United, Champion, A Love of Thunder, Tom's Hand

Image Credits:

All illustrations by Jon Chaiet

p.67 iStock/Copyright: Vincent Shane Hansen
p. 75 iStock/Copyright: EOPITZ
p. 123 and 145 iStock/Copyright: sturti
p. 157 iStock/Copyright: mediaphotos
p. 162 iStock/Copyright: IS_ImageSource
All other images are used under official license from Shutterstock.com

Printed in China

1 2 3 4 5 6 7 8 9 0

First Edition

TABLE OF CONTENTS

REDNECK RIVIERA - 60

Boilermaker	Morning Dew	Mama's Peach Pie
Jägerbomb	Comfy Chair	Redneck Knockout
Cidermeister	Redneck Lemonade	
Surfing USA	Mama's Apple Pie	

PERFECT FOR LOUNGING - 76

Bourbon Sweet Tea	French Toast Eggnog	Ruby Ruby
Long Island Iced Tea	Cosmopolitan	Summer Shandy
Gin and Tonic	Sea Breeze	
Vanilla Eggnog	Rum Chocolate	

DRINKS TO IMPRESS - 92

Classic Old Fashioned	Privateer
Simple Manhattan	Gimlet
Vodka Martini	Moscow Mule
White Russian	Mint Julep
Tequila Sunrise	Sorta Piña Colada

INTRODUCTION

When you think of red plastic cups, what comes to mind? College parties? Raucous tailgates? Apartment parties or backyard BBQs?

All of these answers are right. America is a Red Cup Nation, and these big plastic cups are a symbol of a carefree attitude, laid back lifestyle, and, above all else, a love of booze and hatred of pretention.

After all, it's hard to be pretentious when holding a plastic cup. That's why *Red Cup Nation* features cocktail recipes perfect for gatherings of all shapes and sizes. The red cup keeps everyone on an even playing field. How do you approach a wine snob holding a snifter of Chardonnay? Or the bourbon snob, drinking his Maker's Mark neat in a glass you've never seen before? No, says the red cup. We are the same, you and I. And whether you're sipping on a simple rum and Coke or pouring from the punch bowl, the red cup says we're all here for the same thing: to have fun.

You won't find many complicated recipes in this book, and you definitely won't need a blender, strainer, ice luge, or dictionary to mix them up. Featuring 100 different drinks for every occasion (not to mention a host of both new and classic drinking games), *Red Cup Nation* sets aside the unnecessary pompousness of the average cocktail book to remind us that when it comes to drinking, only two things matter: great taste and good times.

BUCKLE UP!!!

PARTY MIXES

Whether you're throwing a college party in the basement of a fraternity house or throwing a block party for the entire neighborhood, one thing becomes vitally important: providing enough booze to keep everyone satisfied. After all, there's nothing worse than running out of alcohol halfway through a party, right?

Almost as bad is the thought of running out of mixers. Not many people will be thrilled if all you have left is a liter of gin and a pile of empty tonic bottles. Much better to pre-mix your drinks and keep the punch bowl, water cooler, trash can, or other serving vessel you've chosen full.

Naturally, you want your guests coming back for more. Party mixes need to taste great and have a broad appeal—no niche drinks, licorice liqueur, or expensive scotches here. In this section, you'll find drinks with vodka, rum, tequila, gin, and more, all designed to tantalize the taste buds of even the most stubborn partygoers. Alcohol isn't the key to a good time...but it will definitely help open the door.

JUNGLE PUNCH

Everyone knows the term "jungle juice," and if you've ever been to a college party there's a good chance you've consumed more than a bit of it yourself. Really, jungle juice is just a catch-all term for the mismatched slurry of flavors and alcohols served up at any party. For some people, there's a nostalgic feeling when it comes to jungle juice, but not much else. But it doesn't have to be this way! There's no reason the punch at your party shouldn't taste as great as possible.

3 PARTS FRUIT PUNCH	1 PART SPRITE	1 PART VODKA

1. Fill a punch bowl or other large container with ice. Add the vodka and Sprite.
2. Top with fruit punch and stir together until thoroughly mixed. Enjoy!

VARIATIONS

Vodka is best because it takes to the flavor of the other ingredients so well and has a broader appeal. That said, white rum or gin will also work just fine.

What is a "part?" In most of the recipes in this book, you'll see measurements like "1 part this, 2 parts that." This isn't laziness (well, it's not ALL laziness)—it's to help you. Why tie you down to specific measurements? Who wants to measure out precisely 1.5 ounces of booze? We all know you're just going to eyeball it anyway, so relative measurements make everything easy. A "part" is however much you want it to be. Two "parts" is double that. And so on. So if your drink is "one part vodka, two parts club soda," just add twice as much club soda as vodka. Simple!

TEQUILA GRAPEFRUIT

¡MUY BUENO!

Tequila is perfect for parties. It has a distinct taste, but can also be hidden behind other, more flavorful ingredients in a way that will satisfy both tequila lovers and tequila newbies. One of the most powerful such flavors is grapefruit juice. Long a favorite cocktail mixer, grapefruit juice plays nicely off the tasty tequila for a sweet and sour taste that partygoers will love.

**3 PARTS
GRAPEFRUIT JUICE**

**1 PART
SILVER TEQUILA**

**1 PART
SPRITE**

**2 LEMONS
(GARNISH)**

1. Fill a punch bowl or other large container with ice. Add the tequila and Sprite.

2. Top with grapefruit juice and stir together until thoroughly mixed.

3. If you want to make it look nice, slice a few lemons into circles and add them to the bowl. Enjoy!

VARIATIONS

This drink also works very well with vodka or rum. The versatility of grapefruit juice means it mixes with just about anything.

Should you ever want proof that the red cup is an integral and celebrated part of Americana, look no further than the song "Red Solo Cup," written and performed by famed country artist Toby Keith. The song perfectly sums up what this red cup nation loves about its most beloved item of drinkware.

RUNAWAY RUM RUNNER

Say that five times fast. Better yet, wait until after you've had a few of these! A classic Rum Runner cocktail usually contains spiced rum, blackberry liqueur, banana liqueur, orange juice, and grenadine...but who has the time or money for all those ingredients? Let's just take the basic flavors and see if we can't whip up something big that people will love. With a little spiced rum, orange juice, and cran/raspberry juice, you might not have a Rum Runner, but you'll have something that might go down even easier.

---

1 PART SPICED RUM	2 PARTS ORANGE JUICE	1 PART CRAN/ RASPBERRY JUICE

1. Fill a punch bowl or other large container with ice. Add the rum and orange juice.

2. Top with cran/raspberry juice. Don't stir—just let the red coloration seep into the drink.

3. Start serving and enjoy!

VARIATIONS

If you do have banana or blackberry liqueur, by all means add it in. No need for grenadine though—the cran/raspberry juice will add all the color you need and the subtle flavor of the grenadine would be lost against it.

LEMONADE MIX-UP

Alright, so you have a bunch of different liquors lying around but only a little of each. No problemo! Run to the corner store, grab some lemonade and cranberry juice, and mix up a batch of Lemonade Mix-Up. It's quick and easy, and saves you a trip to the liquor store. Gin, vodka, and rum all play well off one another, and hidden behind the sweet lemonade and bitter cranberry, this is a colorful party drink that packs a flavorful punch.

**1 PART
VODKA**

**1 PART
RUM**

**1 PART
CRANBERRY JUICE**

**1 PART
GIN**

**3 PARTS
LEMONADE**

1. Fill a punch bowl or other large container with ice. Add the vodka, gin, and rum.

2. Add the cranberry juice and stir together until thoroughly mixed.

3. Top with lemonade and stir again, until the color is even throughout. Enjoy!

VARIATIONS

You can try making this drink with whiskey or tequila, but be aware that the flavor of the tequila might overpower it and the color of the whiskey might result in something unpleasant looking. Also, as noted before, stay away from spiced rum! It will markedly affect both the flavor AND color.

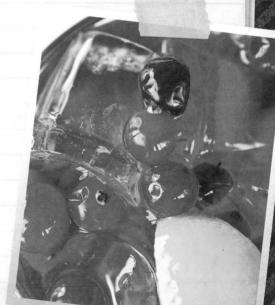

AWE YISS

TROPICAL RUM PUNCH

Rum always makes me think of the beach, or at least the summer. In fact, the only thing that makes me feel more tropical than regular rum is coconut rum. And while I might not be the biggest rum fan in the world myself, I can't deny the delicious flavor that a nice pour of coconut rum can add to even the simplest drinks. This Tropical Rum Punch mix is simple, tasty, and stronger than you think.

**1 PART
WHITE RUM**

**1 PART
ORANGE JUICE**

**PINEAPPLE RINGS
(GARNISH)**

**1 PART
COCONUT RUM**

**1 PART
PINEAPPLE JUICE**

1. Fill a punch bowl or other large container with ice. Add the white and coconut rum.

2. Add the orange juice and pineapple juice, then stir together until thoroughly mixed.

3. To liven things up, slice a pineapple into rings and add them to the bowl as a nice-looking garnish. Enjoy!

VARIATIONS

For a cloudier, darker drink, you can use dark rum in place of white rum. Avoid spiced rum, though—its harsh flavor will clash with the coconut rum.

Solo Cup Co., makers of the most recognizable brand of party cups, say that about 60% of all cups they sell are red. This is primarily because, as with a bullfighter's red cape, the red color of the cups brings out the fun, aggressive, thrill-seeking side of anyone who sees them, resulting in quite the party for all involved.*

*not actually true

DANGER

I really wasn't sure what to call the first Everclear drink in this book, but that seems to get the message across pretty clearly, wouldn't you say? Everclear is (and I cannot stress this enough) strong. Very strong. Rocket fuel-strong. We're talking about a 190-proof alcoholic nightmare that you could probably run a car on. Of course, that's what makes it such an appealing party mixer: bang for your buck. It doesn't taste good, but as long as you mask it with enough mixers, you're golden. Just be careful with your ratios, because a drink with too much Everclear in it is more than a party foul: it's a health hazard for you or anyone else who drinks it.

----

1 PART EVERCLEAR	1 PART GINGER ALE	4 PARTS HAWAIIAN PUNCH

1. Dump some ice into your chosen vessel. Add the ginger ale. I'll be honest: the main reason I'm telling you to add the ginger ale first is because I don't trust you to mix well, and I don't want the bottom of this drink to be an Everclear bomb waiting to go off.

2. Add the Everclear and Hawaiian Punch, then stir together until thoroughly mixed. I mean it. Everything should be thoroughly mixed.

Leave a cup floating on top of your punch concoction so that people can use it to fill their own drinks. After all, you don't want people dipping their own drinks into the punch. They'll get sticky and disgusting. And who needs a ladle when you've got perfectly good cups sitting around?

WHISKEY DANGER

TASTY! ✦✦✦✦✦

Ever had a Whiskey Sour? This is kind of like that. Except instead of a refined drink that you might order at an upscale cocktail bar, the Whiskey Danger is a party drink designed to be made in large batches and kick off a great night the right way. Whiskey tends to get overlooked when it comes to large-batch cocktails, and this is kind of a pity. Because when it's paired with the right mixers, the taste of whiskey, which some might find unappealing on its own, can be a great accent.

1 PART WHISKEY	3 PARTS LEMONADE	1 PART CRANBERRY JUICE

1. Toss some ice into your container of choice. Add the lemonade and whiskey. Stir it up!

2. Top with a little cranberry juice. The color of the whiskey can leave the lemonade looking a little muddy, so the cranberry juice not only adds flavor, but makes the color into something a little more palatable. Stir again and enjoy!

If you're ever worried about your jungle juice looking, well, gross, remember that dark red drinks are your friend. Cranberry juice and fruit punch are additions that work with just about anything and their coloration is so dark that they'll often take over the drink completely. You can also keep some grenadine around. Grenadine is just as capable of adding color to your drinks and has an extremely mild flavor.

JUNGLE JAM

It's punch with a little bit of fizz and a whole lot of kick. Basically, you're using a bottle each of Everclear, triple sec, peach schnapps, and Sprite, and then doubling up those amounts with both Hawaiian Punch and Sunny D. The result is sweet, colorful, fizzy, and STRONG. It's a drinkable party punch that everyone will love for both its taste and its strength.

---

1 PART **EVERCLEAR**	**1 PART** **PEACH SCHNAPPS**	**2 PARTS** **HAWAIIAN PUNCH**
1 PART **TRIPLE SEC**	**1 PART** **SPRITE**	**2 PARTS** **SUNNY D**

1. Literally dump everything together in your serving container. Just dump it all in.
2. Mix it all up, add some ice, and you're good to go.

So you've heard of people using a trash can to make a giant batch of jungle juice, but you're not quite sure how to go about it. No problem. It really isn't hard at all. Just take a large garbage can and line it with food-grade plastic. You can order food-grade plastic sheets online, or you can likely find them at any hardware store. Secure it in place, whip up a huge batch of whatever jungle juice you want, and you're golden. Toss an extra cup in there to serve with, keep a ladle nearby, or hey, get some PVC piping and make a giant straw!

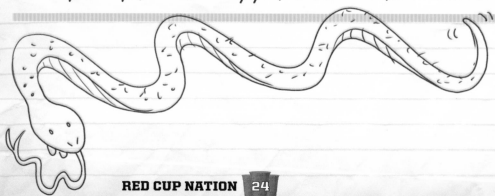

PARTY PUNCH
(AKA DUMP THE LEFTOVERS)

What do you do when you have a bunch of different liquors, a bunch of different mixers, and no real plan? Just throw it all together in a punch bowl and see what happens. Party Punch is simple because there really aren't any hard rules: just throw together everything you've got and pray to the good lord that it will turn out alright. Still, I guess it helps to have a GENERAL idea of what you're doing. Let's see...

**1 PART
VODKA**

**1 PART
GIN**

**1 PART
SOMETHING FIZZY**

**2 PARTS
LEMONADE**

**1 PART
CRANBERRY JUICE**

1. Take what you've got and throw it all together. What's the worst that can happen? Make sure you include some ginger ale or Sprite (or something along those lines) to give it a little fizz. You can hide a lot of shortcomings behind a little fizz.

2. Mix it all up and give it a taste. Is it bad? Hopefully not! But if it is, just tweak it a little bit until you get something drinkable, and you're golden.

VARIATIONS

Haven't you been listening? This recipe IS a variation. Don't have vodka? Fine, use rum. Don't have cranberry juice? Whatever, use fruit punch. As long as you aren't just filling a bowl with Everclear and poisoning your party guests, use your better judgment.

THE SLAMMER

Ever heard of an Alabama Slammer? It's a drink people mostly tend to order in bars, and even then not so much anymore. Regardless of how unpopular it might be now, people loved it back in the day, because it's delicious. The Slammer is something of a departure from the traditional Alabama Slammer, made for large batches and long nights. Heavy on both booze content and flavor, this one is a party keeper.

----

1 PART **VODKA**	**1 PART** **SOUTHERN COMFORT**
1 PART **AMARETTO**	**3 PARTS** **ORANGE JUICE**

1. Pour everything into your container and stir it until it's nice and consistent.

2. Put some ice out for this one. You don't want to put it directly into the bowl where it will melt and water down the drink, but it might be nice to have some nearby.

Keeping ice handy is often a good idea. If you fill your punch bowl (or whatever) with ice, it's going to melt and water down the drink. For some jungle juice batches, that doesn't really matter. But for others, do your party guests a favor and keep the ice off to the side in a cooler.

ONE GIANT KINDA MAI TAI

Mai Tai's are great because they're drinkable. They're also very easy to mix up in large batches, which make them the perfect basis for a jungle juice recipe. This kinda-sorta Mai Tai lacks (let's be honest) all of the subtlety of flavor of a traditional Mai Tai. Instead, it packs a boozy wallop and a drinkable flavor. Who needs subtlety when you've got a ten-gallon trash can to fill?

**1 PART
SPICED RUM**

**1 PART
COCONUT RUM**

**2 PARTS
PINEAPPLE JUICE**

**2 PARTS
ORANGE JUICE**

1. Add ice to your container and start adding ingredients.
2. Once you've added everything together, stir it up and start serving. Enjoy!

VARIATIONS

If you want to darken the color to be a little closer to that of a traditional Mai Tai, add some grenadine or even a little bit of cranberry juice.

ELECTRO PUNCH

You know what's a good color? Blue. Who doesn't love blue? It's the color of the sky. The color of the ocean. And the color of Blue Curaçao, which is a great little boozy addition to a lot of jungle juices. Don't you get tired of the same old red, orange, yellow, or even brown color that jungle juice tends to take on? Electro Punch is a MAJOR departure from that, with an electric blue hue that will certainly draw your eye.

---

1 PART VODKA

1 PART BLUE CURAÇAO

1 PART COCONUT RUM

4 PARTS LEMONADE

1. Add the vodka, coconut rum, and Blue Curaçao to your container and mix them up.

2. Top with the lemonade and mix again. If the color fades too much, feel free to add a little more Blue Curaçao—but don't make the mistake of forgetting that it has alcohol in it. You don't want to overdo it.

Need some good party theme ideas? Decade themes are always fun ('70s, '80s, '90s, or hey, even '00s). You can opt for the ever popular stoplight party (green clothing = single, red clothing = taken, yellow clothing = keeping options open) or go a more formal route with a black tie theme. Complementary themes are great (bikini babes and surfer bros, cowboys and cowgirls, etc.), as are antagonistic themes (cops and robbers, cats and dogs). Just be creative and you're sure to come up with something. When in doubt, just think of something you'd like to see other people dressed as and go from there.

KEEP IT TROPICAL

It's a pretty straightforward batch of red jungle juice, with the addition of a pineapple twist. The pineapple flavors add a nice little tinge of sourness to the concoction, which is a good change of pace from the usual fruit punch based jungle juices. Don't get me wrong, fruit punch is still a great base—but this has a little more depth that partygoers will surely appreciate. And if not, well, too bad. It's your party and you get to decide.

1 PART PINEAPPLE VODKA

2 PARTS FRUIT PUNCH

1 PART PINEAPPLE JUICE

1 PART WHITE RUM

1 PART CRANBERRY JUICE

1. Don't be shy. Fill a punch bowl or other large container with ice and then toss everything together and mix it on up.

2. Honestly, that's all there is to it. I'm at a loss for what "step two" might be. I guess if you have some lime juice handy, you could add a little of that? You don't have to though. Totally your call.

VARIATIONS

Like I said, go ahead and add some lime juice if you've got some lying around. But you'll probably have to add quite a bit for the flavor to come through in a batch as big as this. If you have some fresh pineapple, it might be cool to slice it into rings and let them float in the punch bowl.

TEQUILA MONSTER

RAWR!

Did you get that the name is supposed to sound like "Gila Monster?" No? Fine, screw you! Maybe that was only funny to me. Anyway, Margaritas are awesome, but there's no reason you can't capture a little of that same flavor and make it into a large batch drink. The Tequila Monster captures everything you love about Margaritas and amps it up just a little bit. Half the class, but double the flavor! That's always been my motto.

---

1 PART
GOLD TEQUILA

1 PART
ORANGE JUICE

1 PART
PINEAPPLE JUICE

LIME JUICE
TO TASTE

1. Fill a punch bowl or other large container with ice. Add the tequila, pineapple juice, and orange juice together and stir until they're thoroughly mixed.

2. Add as much lime juice as you need to get that hint of lime flavor that makes Margaritas so great. It can be hard to judge how much you need in a sizeable batch, so just keep adding lime juice and stirring until it tastes right.

OCEAN BREEZE

What's more refreshing than a sea breeze? An ocean breeze, of course. The Sea Breeze is a popular cocktail, but when we're talking about something that can be made in batches large enough to fill a bathtub, it's only fitting to give it a few tweaks and rename it the Ocean Breeze. With a little vodka and gin and that bite that comes with a splash of grapefruit juice, this is a great (and refreshing) party drink.

1 PART VODKA	1 PART GRAPEFRUIT JUICE	3 PARTS CRANBERRY JUICE
1 PART GIN	1 PART SPRITE	

1. Go ahead and toss some ice in this one, it doesn't matter. Then add everything but the Sprite and stir.

2. Top with the Sprite for a little fizz. Mix it up if you want or leave it as is.

Did you know that the lines on a standard Solo cup are there for measurement purposes? It's true! The first line from the bottom denotes 1 oz., slightly less than a standard shot. The 2nd line marks 5 oz., while the third line marks 12 oz., which is the perfect size for a beer. This is handy, because it can help you measure your drinks and keep track of your consumption.

12 oz.

5 oz.

1 oz.

SWEET AND SOUR

Sticking with the grapefruit theme, why not build off what we just did and mix up something that packs a powerful sweet and sour punch? Mix a little grapefruit juice and pineapple juice with some Everclear and peach schnapps and we've got ourselves a party. This is one where you DEFINITELY want to be careful with your alcohol intake. These babies go down so easily you might lose track.

**1 PART
EVERCLEAR**

**2 PARTS
PINEAPPLE JUICE**

**1 PART
PEACH SCHNAPPS**

**2 PARTS
GRAPEFRUIT JUICE**

1. Fill a punch bowl or other large container with ice, pour in the ingredients, and mix it all up.

2. Give it a taste and add some more peach schnapps if you think it needs it. You just want a little of that flavor to come through.

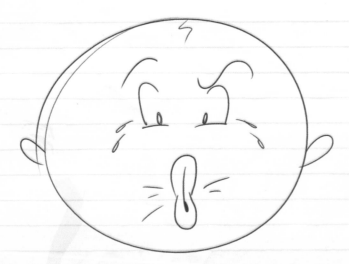

Building a party playlist can be a pain, but it's easier if you pick a theme and stick with it. If you want a mix of club-ready music, check out some popular remixes and EDM music. If you're having a themed party, maybe you want an 80's or 90's playlist. It's easy to consult the old Billboard charts to see what songs were popular when, so that's a good place to begin. The great thing about having so many streaming music services available today is that there are always a million different playlists to choose from, so you can browse them for inspiration if you get stuck.

JUICE BOX

You know what's good? Sangria. You know what people look at you weirdly for drinking anytime after noon? Also Sangria. Which really isn't fair. Sangria is delicious. It's refreshing. It's basically wine with a little extra kick. What's wrong with having some after the sun goes down? Regardless, the Juice Box is a compromise we can all live with. A little red wine, a little fruit juice, and a pop of brandy make a surefire recipe for deliciousness.

**1 PART
BRANDY**

**1 PART
SPRITE**

**2 PARTS
ORANGE JUICE**

**2 PARTS
RED WINE**

**1 PART
CRANBERRY JUICE**

**ASSORTED
FRUIT CHUNKS**

1. Mix the brandy, wine, and juices together with some ice.

2. Top with the Sprite and stir again. Toss some pineapple slices and other fruit chunks in there just like you would with Sangria, if you want.

STORM PUNCH

Simple mixes are often the best, and the Storm Punch mix is about as simple as it gets. Many different cocktails have made use of the dark rum and ginger beer combination, but ginger beer is a little too harsh for a big batch like this. Instead, we'll swap it out for ginger ale and add some orange juice. The result is a drink that more or less answers the question "what would happen if a Dark & Stormy and a Mimosa had a baby?"

**1 PART
DARK RUM**

**1 PART
GINGER ALE**

**1 PART
CHAMPAGNE**

**2 PARTS
ORANGE JUICE**

1. Add ice to your container of choice and mix the ginger ale, champagne, and orange juice.

2. Top it off with the dark rum and stir again. Enjoy!

Champagne is an important ingredient to remember, and it's always smart to keep a bottle on hand. If you want to add a little fizz to you drink while also bumping up the alcohol content, why not add champagne? It has all the fizz of Sprite or ginger ale, along with a nice boozy burn.

PARTY LIKE YOUR BANK ACCOUNT SAYS $19.99

Okay, so you're looking to throw a party but you aren't sure what you need to buy. You don't necessarily have a theme, you just want some cool stuff to give the party a little ambiance...but without spending much money.

The good news is that it isn't as hard as it sounds. Or as expensive. For less than 30 bucks, you can pick up a sack full of goodies that will brighten up the party and leave you plenty of money to spend on booze.

Here's a quick rundown of party favors to take your shindig to the next level:

NEON STRAWS: Nope, I'm not joking. And I'm not saying you have to use them. But when you mix up a vodka and soda for a friend, this will add a nice little pop of color and personality to an otherwise pretty boring drink. And they're cheap! You can pick up well over 100 for as little as **$3**. *Party Cost So Far: $3*

COLORFUL LIGHT BULBS: You'd be surprised how much of a difference it can make, just throwing in a pink or blue light bulb every so often. Strobe lights are expensive, and the more you drink the more dangerous they get. But setting the mood with a little colorful lighting? Well, you can get that for as little as **$1.50** a bulb. Let's be generous and pick up a four pack. *Party Cost So Far: $9*

CHRISTMAS LIGHTS: Now we're thinking outside the box. You might not want to replace every light in your house with a colored light bulb, but you probably don't want to keep all the lights on anyway. Instead of harsh, overhead lighting, why not string some Christmas lights around the room to give it a soft, intimate feeling? You can grab them for **$5** a string, so let's get two. *Party Cost So Far: $19*

CUSTOM PONG BALLS: What could be better than having ping-pong balls emblazoned with your school, fraternity, or house logo? You might have to buy them in bulk, but it's worth the investment. You'll only have to pay about **$1** per ball, so let's pencil you in for ten. *Party Cost So Far: $29*

There you have it. Just four simple ideas and your party is already looking about a million times better. And it only cost you **$29!** Just think how much extra beer you can buy with the leftover cash.

Now, if you REALLY want to go all out, we can start talking about fog machines and laser shows...

MELTED CREAMSICLE

Who doesn't love creamsicles? Aliens, probably (but if we're being honest, that's probably just because Mars has no oranges. Or cows). But everyone else loves them. There's something about that combination of orange and cream that just makes everything better. But why would you eat a creamsicle when you can DRINK one instead? The Melted Creamsicle party punch will hit you hard with its alcohol level, but it will also fill you with nostalgia. Why Sunny D instead of regular orange juice? Hey, if you think the creamsicles you used to eat were made with real orange juice, I've got a bridge to sell you in Brooklyn.

**1 PART
EVERCLEAR**

**2 PARTS
VANILLA VODKA**

**1 PART
TRIPLE SEC**

**6 PARTS
SUNNY D**

1. Pour the Sunny D and vanilla vodka into your container and mix them together.
2. Add in the Everclear and triple sec and stir thoroughly (and I do mean thoroughly—dipping into a layer of Everclear will ruin your night real quick).
3. Taste it—if you can taste the Everclear, add more Sunny D. Always be mindful.

VARIATIONS

If the orange flavor is too overpowering for you or you're looking for an easy way to cut back on the alcohol content, drop the triple sec. It has a little bit more of an orange bite than the Sunny D, but it isn't totally necessary.

NATTY-ADE

Did you know that you can mix beer and lemonade and it'll actually wind up tasting pretty okay? It's the truth, believe it or not. The last party mix here is one that sounds a little unusual, but has become pretty commonplace on college campuses. It shouldn't be a surprise—is it really that different from the hard lemonade craze? Adding a little bit of vodka to the equation makes it even stronger. Oh, and one pro tip: use pink lemonade. Trust me, the color won't be particularly appetizing if you don't.

---

1 CASE OF NATTY LIGHT (OR SIMILAR CHEAP BEER)

2 CONTAINERS OF POWDERED PINK LEMONADE (19 OZ. EACH)

1 HANDLE OF VODKA

1 GALLON OF WATER

1. Add the beer, vodka, and water to your container and mix it all to-gether. It might seem sacrilegious to add ice to beer, but you should add some ice to this drink, too.

2. Add in the powdered lemonade mix and stir it up. If the taste is over-powering, add more water and continue to stir until the powder is completely dissolved.

VARIATIONS

You can adjust the amount of lemonade powder to your particular tastes. Chances are you'll need quite a bit of it to overcome the flavor of the beer, though.

WHEN LIFE GIVES YOU POWDERED LEMONS:
MAKE DRINKS!!!

TAILGATE CLASSICS

Whether you're watching the game on a couch or lounging on the back of a pickup in the stadium parking lot, drinking is a part of sports culture (do people tailgate for things other than sports? Whatever). Some drinks and cocktails have become tailgate fixtures, and these are the ones you should have in your back pocket to whip out before the big game.

Some of these are more complicated than others, but the important thing is that most of them are mobile and all of them are delicious. These are drinks to have with tailgate food: burgers, sausages, wings, pizza, and the rest. They go great with greasy food and, believe me, none of them are particularly good for you. After all, you're going to a game. A tailgate isn't about counting calories. It's about FLAVOR. And these drinks have flavor in spades.

So grab a blender and a handful of red cups and meet me outside the stadium. We'll be pouring drinks right up until kickoff. Because let's face it: who wants to watch the game sober?

MARGARITA

Let's start with the classic to end all classics: the Margarita. It's simple, it's tasty, and it'll almost make you forget that you're drinking tequila, which should really be reclassified as a mind-altering drug. The Margarita is really just three ingredients, all of which you should try to keep stocked at all times. Yes, the Frozen Margarita is more popular, and we'll get to that in a second. But in a pinch, a regular Margarita is a perfectly acceptable and delicious tailgate sipper.

**2 PARTS
GOLD TEQUILA**

**1 PART
TRIPLE SEC**

**1 PART
LIME JUICE**

SALT

1. Add some ice to your cup and build in the other ingredients. Stir it up.
2. Normally you would rim the glass with salt. But we're talking about red cup life here. Forget rimming. You know the trick where you lick salt off your hand before a tequila shot? Just do that. It's easier.

VARIATIONS

There are a billion Margarita variations, most of which involve simply adding a liqueur. Got some raspberry or apple liqueur you want to add in? Be my guest.

FROZEN MARGARITA

This is the most complicated drink I'll have you make: the Frozen Margarita. I thought about not including it, but it just goes too damn well with tailgate foods like tacos and taquitos. I mean, what good is a plateful of tacos without a top shelf Marg to wash it down? Yeah, you'll need a blender, but believe me: you can find a cheap blender that runs on batteries.

**2 PARTS
GOLD TEQUILA**

**1 PART
TRIPLE SEC**

**1 PART
LIME JUICE**

ICE

SALT

1. Add the ingredients to the blender (use about a cup of ice per serving). Blend it all up until it's relatively smooth.

2. Either rim the glass with salt or just do the whole dump-salt-on-your-hand-and-lick-it-off thing. Pour in your Margarita and enjoy.

WHISKEY SOUR

The Whiskey Sour is a time-honored cocktail that you'd think would be complicated. But when you boil it down, it really isn't. Forget the simple syrup that it usually calls for: you don't need it. Forget the orange garnish: it's unnecessary. Just whiskey, lemon juice, and a little sugar and water are all you need. If you are smart enough to keep some maraschino cherries around, you can dress it up a little bit. But really, this is a strong tailgate drink that will wake you up and keep you going all game long. Game about to start? This is a drink you can stick right into your flask.

| 2 PARTS WHISKEY | 1 SPLASH WATER | 1 MARASCHINO CHERRY (GARNISH) |
| 1 PART LEMON JUICE | 1 PINCH SUGAR | |

1. Add some ice to your cup and pour in the ingredients. Stir it up until it's all mixed together.

2. Pop in a maraschino cherry for garnish if you have one (the added benefit here is that when you're done, you get to eat the whiskey-soaked cherry). Otherwise, enjoy it as-is.

SCREWDRIVER

This drink is a toss-up between a morning cocktail and a tailgate drink. On the one hand, it's mostly orange juice. On the other hand, it's easy to make, easy to drink, and easy to share, which makes it great for tailgates. Actually, come to think of it, most tailgating tends to happen in the morning. It's the perfect compromise! Wake up with a few Screwdrivers and by the time the game kicks off you'll feel like you're soaring high above the clouds.

- -

1 PART
VODKA

3 PARTS
ORANGE JUICE

1. Add some ice, then mix the ingredients together. Look, you can make this drink as strong as you want, but I'm going to do the responsible thing here and recommend that you don't go too much stronger than a 3:1 ratio. You're probably going to drink a lot of these, so keep it reasonable.

2. Stir everything up and enjoy!

VARIATIONS

With a little vanilla vodka, you can do great things. Take the next drink, for example...

CREAMSICLE

Earlier I introduced you to the Melted Creamsicle, a large-batch monstrosity designed to keep an entire party happy. Here, I'll keep it a little smaller, and introduce you to the basic Creamsicle, the companion drink to the Screwdriver. Another orange juice-based drink perfect for your morning tailgate, the Creamsicle adds a little extra vanilla flavor. It still isn't an incredibly strong drink, which is probably for the best: you don't want to wind up taking off your shirt and running onto the field before halftime (after halftime, all bets are off).

---

1 PART
VANILLA VODKA

3 PARTS
ORANGE JUICE

1. Add ice to your drink and pour in the ingredients. Stir it up.

2. If the vanilla flavor isn't coming through, feel free to add a bit more. Just be mindful of how much booze you're including and enjoy!

WHISKEY LEMONADE

Hear me out, now. Once, when I was in college, I had a bottle of whiskey and nothing to mix it with. So I wandered downstairs to the vending machines, where, much to my dismay, everything was sold out. Everything, that is, except a bottle of pink lemonade. Well, I didn't have any other option, and I definitely wasn't going to drink my whiskey straight, so I bit the bullet and bought it. I will forever be grateful for that day, because it introduced me to a combination that never would have occurred to me on its own, but has since become one of my game day staples.

---

3 PARTS PINK LEMONADE

1 PART WHISKEY

1. Scoop some ice into your cup and add the ingredients.
2. Stir everything together and enjoy!

ANOTHER ONE!!

JACK AND COKE

K.I.S.S. Keep It Simple, Stupid. Maybe the number one drink at every college bar, the simple Jack and Coke is a no-brainer combination that anyone with even the barest affinity for whiskey will love. It's quick. It's easy. And there's no pressure to do anything special with it. It's a drink without frills or pretention. It's the Gin and Tonic's shadowy companion. The Jack and Coke is a tailgate staple that will never, ever die.

1 PART WHISKEY	**3 PARTS COKE**	**1 LIME**

1. Add ice. Add whiskey. Add Coke. It doesn't get much simpler than that.

2. Stir the ingredients together and squeeze a lime slice in. The lime slice isn't mandatory, but it's the key to a great Jack and Coke. If you're planning on making a bunch of these, just grab a lime or two and thank me later.

VARIATIONS

I'm sure I don't need to say this, but Rum and Coke, Vodka and Coke, or even Tequila and Coke are all perfectly acceptable alternatives. They just aren't as good, that's all.

Coke is a fantastic mixer. It's a taste everyone recognizes, and it manages to be distinct without overwhelming. It isn't a great match for a pine-y liquor like gin, but it's an excellent pairing with most dark liquor. It's always handy to have an extra bottle around, because it's the perfect fallback mixer when you're out of everything else.

CINNAMON CIDER

What's the number one tailgating sport? Football. And what season is prime football territory? Fall. So it only makes sense that at least one cider drink makes its way into the tailgate classics section. Cider tends to mix extremely well with whiskey, but it mixes best with cinnamon whiskey. What's better than a cinnamon apple? Drinking a cinnamon apple. This is a VERY boozy concoction that will definitely warm you up.

1 PART FIREBALL CINNAMON WHISKEY	1 PART APPLE LIQUEUR	3 PARTS APPLE CIDER

1. Add ice, if you want it, then pour the ingredients together.
2. Stir everything together and enjoy!

VARIATIONS

Caramel apples are also very good. If cinnamon whiskey isn't your thing, try adding some caramel liqueur instead. Remove the apple liqueur (it will likely overwhelm the caramel flavor) and enjoy!

FALL SHANDY

Okay, one more cider drink. This one is unique because it doesn't actually involve any liquor at all (well, unless you want to add some yourself). Instead it takes the two best fall brews and combines them into one delicious mixture. Pumpkin pie, apple pie...why choose between them when you can have all the flavor of both in one red cup?

- -

1 PART PUMPKIN ALE

1 PART HARD CIDER

1. Crack open a hard cider. Pour it into your cup.

2. Crack open a pumpkin ale. Pour that into your cup, too.

3. You can stir them together if you want, but you can also leave them separate like a Black & Tan.

VARIATIONS

This combination is great on its own, but if you're looking for something with a little more kick, try adding a shot of cinnamon whiskey into the mix. It's a flavor that complements both ingredients extremely well, and will make for a great addition.

BAR SPOON

HAWTHORNE STRAINER

TONGS

JIGGA!

BOTTLE OPENER

MUDDLER

SHAKER

DON'T BE THAT GUY

Look, I'm not saying you need to bust out the cocktail shaker at every gathering to show off your cocktail making skills. In fact, I am specifically telling you NOT to bust out the cocktail shaker at every gathering to show your cocktail making skills.

Don't be that guy.

Nobody likes that guy.

That said, there definitely IS a time and a place to know how to make an amazing cocktail, and learning to use a cocktail shaker and other assorted mixology tools without making a fool of yourself can be worthwhile.

So here are some simple tips that you should probably pound into your brain before you attempt to show off your skills:

• **COCKTAIL SHAKERS ARE DESIGNED TO BE FILLED WITH ICE.** The purpose of shaking a cocktail isn't just to mix it, it's to cool it quickly. Neglect to put ice in your shaker and you'll end up with a thoroughly mixed, thoroughly warm cocktail.

• **YOU CAN MAKE DUE WITHOUT A MUDDLER.** Muddlers are pretty cool. They look professional. But to be honest, you can accomplish the same goal by mashing ingredients with the back of a spoon.

• **A JIGGER IS REALLY JUST A SHOT GLASS.** But way cooler. It measures out 1.5 oz. of booze, so it makes sense to have if you're mixing a specific ratio. Most are double sided, with the other end measuring another, smaller amount.

• **A STRAINER IS THE MOST PROFESSIONAL THING YOU CAN HAVE.** Maybe you don't NEED a strainer. But nothing makes you look like you know what you're doing better than busting out a Hawthorne Strainer.

• **TONGS ARE SANITARY. GET THEM.** If you're adding ice, don't get your grubby fingers all over someone else's drink. Use tongs and at least pretend like you're a civilized person.

NORTH ATLANTIC DEPTH CHARGE

Some of you may know this drink better by another name, but since I'm Irish and I'm the one writing this book, the rest of you will just have to deal with it. The North Atlantic Depth Charge is a St. Patrick's Day favorite, but it's also just the sort of drink that you'd expect to see a bunch of shirtless men painted in team colors downing together. I'm all for responsible consumption and all, but there's just something primal about competing with your friends to see who can down theirs first.

| 1 CAN GUINNESS (OR OTHER STOUT) | ½ SHOT JAMESON IRISH WHISKEY | ½ SHOT BAILEY'S IRISH CREAM |

1. Fill your cup most of the way with Guinness (leave some room at the top).
2. Fill a shot glass with half whiskey, half Irish cream.
3. Drop the shot glass directly into the Guinness and drink it as quickly as possible! The beer will curdle the cream, so you really do want to down this one FAST.

Always keep a shot glass or two or ten with your tailgate kit. It's inevitable: at some point during the day, someone will bust out a bottle of whiskey and demand that everyone do a shot. Not only is it better to be able to have everyone take their shot at the same time, but it also saves you from having to drink directly from the same bottle as everyone else.

REDNECK RIVIERA

Remember the days when "redneck" was an insult? Feels like a million years ago. Now it's more or less a point of pride, a title worn by people who do things their own way, who don't get pushed around, and who like to have a great time. Frankly, it's hard to imagine anyone who embodies the *Red Cup Nation* lifestyle better than the classic American redneck.

We're living in the golden age of the redneck. Even as hipsters take over the cities with their skinny jeans and mason jars, the Redneck Riviera is thriving throughout the country. Who needs to go through the hassle of making a batch of Margaritas or 45 gallons of knockoff Screwdrivers when you can just as easily grab what you've got on hand, mix it on up, and then cast your line right back into the lake? As far as lifestyles go, it's hard to do much better than that.

So I'll just throw a handful of ideas your way. These drinks are simple. They're easy. And they pack a hell of a punch. Whether you're enjoying the sunshine in the backyard with a few friends, heading out to the lake for a day of fishing, or even just working in the garage, these drinks will hit the spot. Some are heavy, some are light, but all of them bring something different to the table.

BOILERMAKER

Let's go ahead and start off with a bang. The Boilermaker is a drink that has probably existed since whiskey and beer were first invented. It's not for the faint of heart. It's the sort of drink that gets your night started quickly and opens your eyes WIDE. There are many different ways to prepare it, but there's really only one right way to drink it.

1 CAN
BEER

1 SHOT
WHISKEY

1. No surprises here. Just pour yourself a full cup of beer and a shot of whiskey.

2. Pour the whiskey directly into the beer and drink it down.

VARIATIONS

If you're REALLY feeling reckless, you can do what I accidentally did the first time I had a boilermaker: chug the drink as if it were a Jägerbomb. Speaking of which...

JÄGERBOMB

You knew it was coming, and what better section to include America's favorite heart attack-inducing monstrosity than right in the heart of the Redneck Riviera? The Jäger-bomb has taken on a life of its own in America's drinking culture as the perfect vehicle for the often-loved, often-reviled Jägermeister liqueur. Some people can't stand it due to its licorice taste, to which I say, who cares? If you can even taste the Jäger when you down this baby, you're doing it WRONG.

----

1 CAN
RED BULL

1 SHOT
JÄGERMEISTER

1. Pour one can of Red Bull directly into your cup (should fill it about halfway).
2. Pour a shot of Jägermeister.
3. Drop the shot of Jägermeister directly into the Red Bull and chug it down.

VARIATIONS

"Bomb" shots are always pretty popular, and they don't take too much creativity. Just take your favorite booze and drop it into something. Hate Red Bull and want to do it with Sprite instead? Do whatever you want. I'm not the boss of you.

CIDERMEISTER

Before we get off the Jägermeister train, let's add in a great little fall drink for the Redneck Riviera. The Cidermeister cocktail usually involves a little coconut rum to damp down the taste of the Jäger, but why bother? Dark liquor just about always goes well with apple cider, which makes anything with Jäger in it a fall cocktail in my book. This is a quick and easy drink that tastes great whether you drink it hot or cold.

----

1 PART JÄGERMEISTER

3 PARTS APPLE CIDER

1. Fill your cup about ¼ of the way with Jäger, then fill the rest with apple cider.
2. If you want, heat it up in the microwave for 30 seconds or so. If you're going to do this, please don't do it in a plastic cup.

VARIATIONS

If you actually do happen to have coconut rum sitting around, add in about half a shot worth. Coconut rum has a very subtle flavor, and sometimes it's nice to have something to temper the harsh taste of the Jäger.

SURFING USA

A lot of people look down on Mountain Dew, and those people are assholes. Objectively, it's a great-tasting drink. Subjectively, it's a great-tasting mixer. Yes, we're back on the Jägermeister wagon, but just for a second! I swear, this will be the last one. In this section, anyway. And this time, you actually do need coconut rum. Or you can just omit it. Whatever. I'm just the guy writing the recipes, who cares what I have to say.

---

1 PART JÄGERMEISTER
1 PART COCONUT RUM
3 PARTS MOUNTAIN DEW

1. Mix the Jäger and coconut rum together in your cup. It should be a little less than half full.

2. Fill the remainder with Mountain Dew and mix it up. The result is a weirdly tropical drink that goes down real easy.

Guys, let's talk about coconut rum. I know, it's kind of a girly thing to keep around (if you're a girl, pretend I didn't say that). But ladies love coconut rum. It's not hard to see why. It's sweet and delicious. So if you want to feel like a genius, just keep an extra bottle of Malibu lying around for when you want to mix up something special for your lady.

MORNING DEW

Remember when Pepsi started putting out those Mountain Dew mixes that were basically half Mountain Dew, half orange juice? I have a feeling that most of you probably never tried those. Well I did, and all I have to say is that shit was DELICIOUS. Which brings us to the Morning Dew, AKA the Redneck Riviera's answer to the boring Screwdriver. The Morning Dew is delicious. It'll wake you up. It'll put your hangover on hold. And it'll go down easy enough that you can drink two or three of them before SportsCenter finishes its first go-around.

1 PART VODKA	1 PART ORANGE JUICE	2 PARTS MOUNTAIN DEW

1. Fill your cup about ¼ of the way with orange juice and ¼ of the way with vodka.
2. Top the rest with Mountain Dew, stir, and enjoy!

VARIATIONS

Don't like vodka? Fine, use rum. This is a pretty adaptable drink, because the flavors of the orange juice and Mountain Dew are probably going to be at the forefront no matter what you do. You could probably even add whiskey to this and it wouldn't taste substantially different.

COMFY CHAIR

Here's another type of booze that doesn't get as much love as it deserves: Southern Comfort. It's rich. It's sweet. And you can even just drink it on its own. But why bother when there are so many great ways to mix it up? Here's a simple drink that you can ease into just like your favorite comfy chair. It goes down smooth and warms you up, and, thanks to the SoCo at its base, it's easy to sip without feeling like you're downing a whole bottle of booze.

1 PART SOUTHERN COMFORT	1 PART VODKA	3 PARTS LEMONADE

1. Add the SoCo and vodka together in your cup until it's a little more than ⅓ of the way full.
2. Top it off with lemonade and mix it up. Enjoy!

REDNECK LEMONADE

On the other hand, who needs SoCo when you've got regular old whiskey? Whiskey and lemonade is a great combination (and was apparently a favorite of Ernest Hemingway's), go figure, right? You just never know who's going to turn out to be a redneck at heart. Perfect for any old summer day, the only thing that could make it better would be to add a little extra booze...so why not go for hard lemonade instead? Beware, though. This packs a much bigger punch than you might expect.

---

1 PART
WHISKEY

3 PARTS
HARD LEMONADE

1. Add ice to your cup and mix together the whiskey and hard lemonade.

2. If you want to cut down on the carbonation, add some regular lemonade as well. Enjoy!

MAMA'S APPLE PIE

How about some more apple cider? After all, what could possibly make you feel more at home in the country than some fresh baked apple pie? Since my baking skills aren't exactly up to scratch (and, now that I think about it, this isn't a cookbook anyway), the best I can do for you is tell you how to make a delicious cocktail that will make you think of mama's best apple pie recipe. It's not the same, but it's pretty damn close.

**1 PART
FIREBALL CINNAMON WHISKEY**

**1 PART
VANILLA VODKA**

**1 PART
APPLE JUICE**

**2 PARTS
APPLE CIDER**

1. Mix the whiskey and vodka together in your glass, then add in the apple juice. Stir them together.

2. Top it off with the apple cider and stir again. Enjoy!

3. If you're feeling REALLY ambitious (or have someone to impress), you can serve it hot and top it with some whipped cream. That'll get you presentation points.

STACK'EM UP!!

BACKYARD
BBQ ETIQUETTE

Whether it's the Fourth of July or just a regular old backyard get-together, BBQs are one of summer's greatest joys. In fact, I would argue that there might not be a better excuse to bust out the red cups, paper plates, and cheap booze than a good old fashioned grill-up-the-hot-dogs backyard bash.

But it's important to remember that there is etiquette. And when it comes to BBQ etiquette, there are a few things you should know.

WHAT SHOULD I BRING? Well, if you're smart, you'll ask the host. If you're dumb, you'll have to figure something out. Rest assured, you can never go wrong bringing booze. If you show up with a handle of whiskey, no one is going to question you.

HOW DRUNK AM I ALLOWED TO GET? Some people would say it's best to play this one by ear, but I'm going to go all in and say "very." It's summer! No one is going to look at you sideways if you fall asleep in the backyard before 8 pm. In fact, I would argue that it's practically expected.

WHAT KIND OF DRINKING GAMES CAN WE PLAY? Some great outdoor games include Beer Pong, Darts, Dodgebeer, and Flip Cup. If you don't know how to play those games, flip forward to the Drinking Games section on page 142.

WHAT SHOULD I WEAR? Kind of a weird question, if you ask me. But since you did ask, a backyard BBQ is the perfect opportunity to bust out that sleeveless tee you've been neglecting. Go ahead. Now is its time to shine.

HOW SHOULD I ORDER MY BURGER? The answer is medium rare. The answer is always medium rare. And make sure you eat as many of them as you can, because you're going to want plenty of food in your stomach for an alcohol-fueled event like this.

YO MAMA'S PEACH PIE

You know what rivals apple pie? Peach pie. Mama's Peach Pie, much like its apple pie cousin, is the next best thing to having a fresh baked pie to sink your teeth into. It's a little more complicated, because you can rarely find straight-up "peach juice," but no matter! What you CAN find is grape/peach juice, and that's just as good. Grape juice makes for such a good mixer that its grapey taste is almost an afterthought, leaving you with the peach flavor you love.

**1 PART
VODKA**

**1 PART
PEACH SCHNAPPS**

**3 PARTS
PEACH/GRAPE JUICE**

**1 PINCH
SUGAR**

1. Add ice to your glass and mix the liquid ingredients together. Stir.
2. Top with a pinch of sugar and stir again. Enjoy!

When it comes to cocktail mixers, grape and cranberry juices are king. And let's face it: today's processed juices seem to last forever. It never hurts to have extra bottles of grape and cranberry juice in your fridge—or even one of the countless combination mixes that populate grocery stores. Grape/cranberry? Peach/grape? Cranberry/cherry? Why not try them all? They all have unique flavors and they'll all mix with a ton of different liquors.

REDNECK KNOCKOUT

This book has been curiously devoid of shots thus far. Let's change that. The Redneck Knockout features three favorites of the Redneck Riviera: whiskey, bourbon, and good old Southern Comfort. Taken together, they make a surprisingly delicious shot. The whiskey and bourbon play off each other in an obvious way, but the addition of the SoCo means there's a little extra sweetness to the shot that makes it that much easier to knock back.

---

1 PART WHISKEY

1 PART BOURBON

1 PART SOUTHERN COMFORT

1. In equal measure, mix all three ingredients together in a shot glass.
2. Knock it back all at once and try not to cry.

PERFECT FOR LOUNGING

Okay. So you don't need a hundred gallons of generic slop to serve at a party. And you don't need a fancy drink to impress anyone, either. You don't want an over-the-top concoction, but you don't want to go overly lowbrow, either. Man, you're picky.

Fortunately for you, I've got the perfect solution: lounge drinks. These are simple drinks (some classic, some not) that are easy to whip up but offer you some semblance of decorum. They're great for backyard barbecues or even just hanging out and watching a baseball game. These are great nightcap drinks, but they're also fantastic dinner drinks. They perfectly walk that middle line between convenience and class, and they're just what you need.

So kick back and relax with these extremely drinkable, non-overthinkable cocktail mixes that will leave you with a pleasant buzz without the need to guzzle grain alcohol. Drinking is supposed to be an enjoyable, social activity, so let's get back to basics.

BOURBON SWEET TEA

Honestly, Bourbon Sweet Tea is best if you make the tea from scratch and boil the bourbon with it. But this is Red Cup Nation! Nobody has time for that. If you have a favorite brand of sweet tea, that'll do just fine to accomplish our goal, which is a delicious and boozy mix that will last you all day long. Can you ever imagine getting tired of a sweet tea-based cocktail? I can't. And until I inevitably die from mainlining this stuff directly into my system, I never will.

1 PART BOURBON	**2 PARTS SWEET TEA**	**1 SQUEEZE LEMON JUICE**

1. Add ice to your cup and pour in the bourbon and sweet tea. Stir them together.
2. Top with a squirt of lemon juice and then stir again. Enjoy!

VARIATIONS

There are a million ways to add a little something to your sweet tea. If lemon juice isn't your thing, try lime juice. Or mint. Or any of a thousand different juices and herbs that add a little bit of flavor to an otherwise straightforward drink.

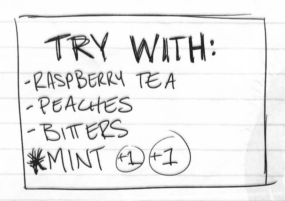

TRY WITH:
- RASPBERRY TEA
- PEACHES
- BITTERS
- *MINT +1 +1

STRONG!

~~LONG~~ ISLAND ICED TEA

The classic. Often imitated, never duplicated: the Long Island Iced Tea. The favorite drink of those who want to get truly sloshed in the least amount of time possible. The undisputed lightweight champion of the world. Sometimes, just sometimes, a drink fails to live up to its outrageous reputation. Not in this case. The Long Island Iced Tea will ruin you FAST. If you're not paying attention to your consumption, you might wind up in bed by 7:00. Then again, if you're cruising through Long Island Iced Teas, maybe that's what you wanted in the first place.

1 PART TEQUILA	1 PART VODKA	1 PART TRIPLE SEC
1 PART GIN	1 PART RUM	2 PARTS COKE

1. Build in all of the alcoholic ingredients and stir them together.
2. Top with a splash of Coke. This should probably make you aware of the fact that this drink is about 99% alcohol. Beware.

It cannot be stressed enough how dangerous drinks like the Long Island Iced Tea are. The Long Island Iced Tea is so named because it tastes like iced tea, despite have exactly zero drops of iced tea in it. Mixing so many different types of liquor together with so little to water it down is always dangerous, so if you're making a drink for someone else, make sure they know exactly what you're giving them.

GIN AND TONIC

Speaking of classic drinks, it's hard to imagine a more straightforward classic than the Gin and Tonic. I grew up drinking them with my family, and now I drink them in every bar, at every wedding, and anytime I have a bottle of gin and nothing but time on my hands. It really is the simplest flavor combination you can imagine, and it's something that fits just about anyone's palate. Even those who don't love gin will often find that the flavor of the added lime makes the whole thing palatable, and sometimes even delicious.

1 PART GIN	2 PARTS TONIC WATER	1 SQUEEZE LIME JUICE

1. Add some ice to your cup and pour in the gin and tonic water. Stir together.
2. Top with a squeeze of lime juice (or even a fresh lime wedge, if you have one) and enjoy!

Fresh lime juice is obviously the best, but keeping limes around can be a pain in the ass. When you don't use an entire lime, it sucks seeing what's left of it wither away in your fridge. So do yourself a favor and pick up one of those lime juice bulbs. You know the ones I mean. They'll last a very long time, and the benefit of having lime juice to add to your Gin and Tonics and other cocktails is immeasurable.

VANILLA EGGNOG

It's a basic fact that rum and eggnog go extremely well together. But while spiced rum runs the risk of overpowering the flavor of the eggnog itself, a little white rum adds just a subtle flavor variant and bite of alcohol. What REALLY takes this drink to the next level is the addition of a bit of vanilla vodka. Eggnog is rich and creamy on its own, but the addition of a little vanilla flavor really takes it to the next level.

1 PART **WHITE RUM**	**1 PART** **VANILLA VODKA**	**3 PARTS** **EGGNOG**

1. Pour the rum and vodka into a glass, then top with eggnog.
2. Stir everything together vigorously. It may take a while before everything mixes together smoothly, so keep at it.

Whether you're personally a fan of eggnog or not, it's a great thing to have handy when the holidays roll around. Whipping up a batch of spiked eggnog is sure to be a festive hit, and the crazy drunk uncle who you only see once a year will look at you with eyes full of wonder the moment you put a pitcher in front of him.

ONE FOR ME...

TWO FOR ME...

MAN WE GOT SOME FORKS SO YOU **KNOW** IT'S A PARTY

PARTY!

FRENCH TOAST EGGNOG

You've already got a few fall and summer drinks to choose from, so let's stick with the winter eggnog theme here. If you like Vanilla Eggnog, you're sure to love French Toast Eggnog. With a little bit of cinnamon and maple flavor as well as a dash of nutmeg, this is the perfect winter warmer to sip when you come in from the cold. Down a couple in front of a cozy fire and you'll feel its effects start to warm you up inside and out.

---

1 PART MAPLE WHISKEY

3 PARTS EGGNOG

1 PART CINNAMON WHISKEY

1 DASH NUTMEG

1. Pour the maple and cinnamon whiskies together into a glass, then top with eggnog.

2. Stir everything together vigorously. It may take a while before everything mixes together smoothly, so keep at it.

If you don't have any maple flavored booze, adding a small splash of maple syrup can sometimes do the trick (as long as you make peace with the fact that it will be a much harder ingredient to combine). This is key, because a little maple flavor can make any drink into a morning drink. And when the holidays roll around and you're in close quarters with your family for weeks at a time, a morning drink or ten will be exactly what you need!

COSMOPOLITAN

This drink might be a little more upscale and Cosmopolitan (IT'S A JOKE, GET IT) than most of the others in this section, but that's mainly because people don't really seem to understand what a Cosmopolitan actually IS. Yes, it's a magazine aimed at women. Yes, the drink is pink. But that doesn't mean that the cocktail itself isn't delicious and worthy of consumption. It's a drink perfect for a Girls Night, that much is true. But it's also a nice Saturday sipper that definitely won't leave you unhappy.

**2 PARTS
VODKA (CHILLED)**

**1 PART
CRANBERRY JUICE**

**1 MARASCHINO
CHERRY (GARNISH)**

**1 PART
TRIPLE SEC**

**1 SPLASH
LIME JUICE**

1. Add the vodka, triple sec, and cranberry juice together and stir. It's a pretty pink drink that would look best in a cocktail glass, but I understand that that's probably a bridge too far.

2. Top with a squirt of lime juice.

3. Garnish with a maraschino cherry. It's not the traditional garnish, but hopefully you have some around to add a little more color.

CHUG, CHUG, CHUG!

Yeah, I know. Sometimes you just want to chug a beer as fast as you can. And you know what? There's nothing wrong with that (well, unless you do too many. Don't do too many, please). But the thing is, there are just so many different WAYS to pour beer into your body as quickly as possible. You've probably heard of a few of them. But what about the ones you haven't?

Let's review.

KEG STAND: Let's start off with a bang. For the uninitiated, a keg stand is when you get a bunch of your friends to pick you up and turn you upside-down (or sideways) over the keg, then you put the nozzle in your mouth, and drink for as long as you can without stopping. Usually accompanied by a chant keeping count.

BEER FUNNEL: Also known as a Beer Bong. It's exactly what it sounds like. Take a funnel. Attach a length of tubing to it. Put the tube in your mouth. Pour beer(s) into the funnel. There you go, a step-by-step guide to beer funneling. Don't you feel dumb for asking?

SHOTGUN: To shotgun a can of beer, start by punching a hole in the side (tip: Take a key and press it parallel to the side of the can using your thumb. Apply a little pressure and it should punch right in easily). Press the hole to your mouth, then pop the top of the can. Down it as quick as you can. Get a few of your friends to do it with you and see who which LOSER takes the longest to finish.

BOMB: Beer and liquor, together at last. There are a few different types of "bombs" (several of which are in this very book), but the basic idea is that you drop a shot of liquor into a pint of beer. Usually you chug the resulting mixture, but if you want to admit that you're bad at drinking you could probably sip it.

SEA BREEZE

Another classic cocktail with a cranberry juice twist, the Sea Breeze is a delicious, summery drink with a satisfying fizz and an even more satisfying pop of citrus. Cranberry juice and lime juice mix astonishingly well, making a fantastic combination perfect for any time of day. I'm serious—whether you're feeling like a boozy brunch or settling down for a Thirsty Thursday evening, the Sea Breeze is guaranteed to hit the spot.

---

1 PART VODKA

2 PARTS CRANBERRY JUICE

1 PART GRAPEFRUIT JUICE

1 SQUIRT LIME JUICE

1. Add ice to your cup, then squirt in the lime juice and vodka.
2. Top off with the cranberry and grapefruit juice.
3. Stir and enjoy!

RUM CHOCOLATE

There just aren't enough hot chocolate-based drinks. It's silly, because hot chocolate is the quintessential winter warmer. It's sweet. It's warm. It's delicious. What could be better than adding a little bit of booze to the equation? When you come in off the slopes, or even after shoveling your driveway, settling down with a nice, warm, chocolaty rum drink is just what the doctor ordered. You may not be able to drink this one out of a red cup, but the spirit is there.

**1 PART
DARK RUM**

**3 PARTS
HOT CHOCOLATE**

**1 HANDFUL
MARSHMALLOWS**

1. Pour the hot chocolate into a mug. Top with dark rum.

2. Add a handful of marshmallows. What's hot chocolate without marshmallows?

RUBY RUBY

Sometimes you just want something bright. Sometimes you just want something sweet. And sometimes you just want something fizzy. The Ruby Ruby can deliver on all three promises, giving you a tasty treat that you and anyone else you serve it to is sure to love. The addition of the club soda really helps this pop, so while you could arguably make a similarly tasty drink without it, I don't recommend leaving it out. Viva la seltzer!

**1 PART
GIN**

**1 PART
CLUB SODA**

**2 PARTS
GRAPEFRUIT JUICE**

**1 PART
TRIPLE SEC**

**1 PART
CRANBERRY JUICE**

1. Add the gin and triple sec together and stir in the club soda.
2. Top with cranberry and grapefruit juice and stir. Enjoy!

SUMMER SHANDY

You've seen the Fall Shandy, now check out its more popular summer cousin. The Summer Shandy is a common enough drink (so much so that if you just order a "Shandy," chances are they'll know what you're talking about), and one that makes for a refreshing option on hot days. It's not high in alcohol content, but sometimes you're not trying to get drunk, you know? Sometimes you just want to sit back with a refreshing drink and slowly build a buzz over the course of a day. I respect that, and you should, too.

---

1 PART
LEMONADE

3 PARTS
WHEAT BEER

1. Fill your cup about ¾ of the way with beer.
2. Top with lemonade and enjoy!

VARIATIONS ← YES!

If you DO want a little extra booze, try adding in a bit of whiskey. If you want to offset the whiskey flavor, a bit of honey will do. Mix all of that up and you'll have yourself a rich and delicious summer slammer.

DRINKS TO IMPRESS

Is there room for a touch of class in the Red Cup lifestyle? Of course there is. Even the most dedicated tailgaters and partiers understand that, every now and then, you've got to step up your game. You've got to put on airs. You've got to *impress*.

No, you don't need to know how to make an "Appletini," and no, you probably aren't going to be whipping up a batch of Strawberry Daiquiris for your next apartment party. But it never hurts to have a fancy drink to whip out when the occasion calls for it. Whether it's the first time your new girlfriend comes home with you, or you just want to know what to order at your best friend's wedding, arming yourself with a little extra knowledge is always a winning strategy.

So keep the Red Cup mindset but set the actual red cups aside for moment. Take a deep breath and plunge into the world of classic drinks. Let people know that, yeah, I clean up real nice when the situation calls for it.

CLASSIC OLD FASHIONED

Let's start simple. If there's one drink that people tend to order when they want to look classy, it's the Old Fashioned. The Old Fashioned is a simple whiskey drink, with a little bit of sugar and bitters added. It's a good-looking drink—especially if you have the right garnishes—and handing someone a properly made Old Fashioned is the sort of thing that will raise an eyebrow or two before they even taste it. Are the garnishes a little much? Maybe. But if you're looking to impress, why not start off right?

---

2 OZ.
BOURBON

1 PINCH
SUGAR

1 SPLASH
WATER

2 DROPS
BITTERS

1 STRIP
ORANGE RIND
(GARNISH)

1 MARASCHINO
CHERRY (GARNISH)

1. Toss a pinch of sugar into your cup or glass. Add the orange rind, a splash of water, and the two drops of bitters, then stir it all together.

2. Fill the glass with ice, then add the bourbon and stir.

3. Garnish with a maraschino cherry if you have one.

VARIATIONS

One of the benefits of the maraschino cherry is that it adds a rosy color to the drink. If you don't have any maraschino cherries but you have a little grenadine lying around, try adding a few drops of it to the mix. It will deepen the color just a bit and add a bit of extra flavor as well.

Fans of Mad Men will no doubt be familiar with the Old Fashioned. The hard-drinking characters on the show are particularly fond of bourbon, and the Old Fashioned is a simple and elegant drink tailor made for television.

SIMPLE MANHATTAN

Sticking with the whiskey theme, let's move on to another drink that people love to order when they want to sound like experts. The Manhattan is colorful, flavorful, and sounds like exactly the sort of thing that a Manhattanite would order. Whether that's true or not doesn't really matter, now does it? These drinks are all about perception. When you want to impress, mixing up a couple of well-made Manhattans will do the trick.

3 PARTS WHISKEY (RYE, IF YOU HAVE IT)

1 PART SWEET VERMOUTH

2 DROPS BITTERS

1 MARASCHINO CHERRY (GARNISH)

1. Add the ingredients together in a glass or cup, then stir them together. Don't be too rough with your stirring or you'll ruin the color.

2. (Optional) If you're feeling really ambitious, you can stir the drink with ice to chill it, then strain it into another cup.

3. Garnish with a maraschino cherry.

Look, garnishes aren't the most necessary addition, but if you're looking to make your drink really "pop" and impress whoever you made it for, it's not a bad idea to keep a jar of maraschino cherries in the fridge. They're one of the most common garnishes, they taste great, they're colorful, and they pretty much last forever, which means you don't have to worry about them going bad.

VODKA MARTINI
(YEAH, LIKE JAMES BOND)

Martinis are simple. Two ingredients, that's it. On the one hand, that makes them great, because they're so easy to whip up. On the other hand, that means you better like the taste of alcohol, because there's not much to mask it in here. If you're a big vodka drinker, go ahead and order a Vodka Martini and see how you like it. Yeah, it's James Bond's favorite drink. Whatever gets your attention, man.

----

3 PARTS VODKA	1 PART DRY VERMOUTH	1 DASH LEMON JUICE

1. Add the vodka and vermouth to your cup, then add a TINY squirt of lemon juice. A typical Vodka Martini is served with a lemon rind, but that might be a bridge too far for us here.

2. Stir together and enjoy.

Legit cocktails usually involve a cocktail shaker or stirring with ice, but that's all kind of a pain in the ass. Remember that you can store clear liquors like vodka and gin in the freezer without fear of them freezing. A chilled Martini is about a million times better than a warm one, so save yourself some effort and just keep the vodka in the freezer.

007 ACTUALLY ORDERS A 'VESPER MARTINI' WHICH CONTAINS LILLET BLANC AS WELL.

WHITE RUSSIAN
(YEAH, LIKE IN *THE BIG LEBOWSKI*)

Thanks the Dude consuming about 100 of them over the course of The Big Lebowski, *the White Russian is a classic drink that's had a little bit of a resurgence lately. That is to say, if you offer someone a White Russian, they'll probably at least know what you're talking about. It's a rich and delicious drink, and it packs so much flavor that you probably won't even realize there's booze in it.*

1 PART VODKA	1 PART COFFEE LIQUEUR	2 PARTS MILK

1. Add some ice to your cup (you have ice, right?), then add in the vodka and coffee liqueur (for the love of God, tell me you have coffee liqueur).
2. Top it off with milk and stir everything together.

VARIATIONS

Some people like to leave the milk on top without stirring. It has kind of a nice look when served in a glass, if you're into that sort of thing. Oh, and it's usually made with cream instead of milk, but I'm just assuming you don't have that much cream lying around.

TEQUILA SUNRISE

I know it's a sacrilege, but for the love of all that is right in the world, please serve this one in a glass. The entire point of the Tequila Sunrise is presentation, so don't screw this one up. There are only a couple of ingredients, and when you put them together in the right order, you get a vibrant and colorful drink that looks kind of like a sunrise. Get it? Good. Because it's a drink that not only looks great, but tastes great, too. And you won't find a better combination for impressing your date when she pops in for a nightcap.

**1 PART
VODKA**

**1 SPLASH
GRENADINE**

**2 PARTS
ORANGE JUICE**

**1 MARASCHINO
CHERRY (GARNISH)**

1. Pay attention to the order here, because it's important. First, add some ice to a glass and pour in the vodka.

2. Now, add orange juice until the glass is ALMOST full.

3. Top with just a SMALL splash of grenadine. Too much and it will over-power the drink and turn the whole thing red. Have a steady hand and add a small splash, and watch it filter down.

4. Garnish with a maraschino cherry if you have one, which you prob-ably don't because you ignored the sidebar I took the time to write about this very topic.

VARIATIONS

The Tequila Sunrise is the most popular, but you can make a Vodka Sunrise if you prefer (obviously just swap out the tequila for vodka). Any clear liquor works, really. If you want to try out a Rum Sunrise or a Gin Sunrise (God help you), go right ahead.

PRIVATEER

Let's come back to coconut rum. The Privateer makes it clear that when I said you should always keep coconut rum on hand, I wasn't kidding. It goes into so many fantastic drinks that having a little bit around will go a long way when you have guests. Whether you want to make some tasty drinks for yourself or you want to whip up a batch when the neighbors come over, the Privateer is a great example of how coconut rum can change the flavor game when it comes to cocktails.

1 PART COCONUT RUM	3 PARTS COKE	1 SPLASH LIME JUICE

1. Add ice to your cup or glass and pour the rum and Coke together.
2. Stir everything until it's nice and mixed, then add a squirt of lime juice. If you have a lime, a nice lime slice would be a sweet garnish.

GIMLET

Yeah, it sounds like a character from The Lord of the Rings, *but it's actually a pretty tasty classic cocktail in the same vein as the Martini. All you need are two simple ingredients, and you've got yourself a drink that will really make you seem like a master mixologist. With nothing but chilled gin and lime juice, the Gimlet is one of those drinks that will really impress people when you make it right.*

---

6 PARTS
GIN

1 PART
LIME JUICE

1. Add the gin to your cup or glass, then top it with a splash of lime.
2. Stir together and enjoy!

VARIATIONS

Like a Martini, the Gimlet is usually served without ice. Sometimes, though, that can leave a drink feeling a little light in your hand. This is the perfect place to make use of whiskey stones, or something similar that won't water down your drink.

DON'T EVEN THINK ABOUT IT

There are certain things you just don't do at a party. You don't do them on purpose. You don't do them by accident. These are the mythical things known as Party Fouls. If you start venturing into party foul territory, you'd best check yourself. If you find yourself unable to STOP committing party fouls, it might be time to go.

Here's a list of just a few party fouls to avoid.

DON'T KNOCK OVER A DRINK. The original party foul. Whether you drop your own drink or knock over someone else's, anything that hits the floor is a waste of booze. You should (and will) be shamed.

DON'T LEAVE WOUNDED SOLDIERS. What's a wounded soldier? Well, that's when you put your half-finished drink down and forget to come back to it. There's nothing worse than picking up half-filled beers during cleanup the next day.

DON'T MESS WITH THE PLAYLIST. Hey, man. It's not your party. You might not like Marky Mark and the Funky Bunch, but apparently the host does, so keep your hands to yourself.

DON'T TAKE PICTURES. Come on. This should be a no-brainer. Everyone likes to get a little sloppy now and then. What they don't like is a reminder of it the next day.

DON'T PASS OUT AT THE PARTY. This probably goes without saying, but unless you've made arrangements to stay over, make sure you're sober enough to get yourself home. No one likes having to rouse the passed out partygoers from their couch at 3 am.

DON'T CREEP. You know what I'm talking about. Don't stare across the room at other partygoers and keep your hands from wandering. If you're making someone visibly uncomfortable, trust me, they're not alone.

DON'T PUKE. Maybe I'm an optimist. I don't know. But I'd like you to at least have the GOAL of not puking. If you must puke, don't do it indoors. And if you must puke indoors, puke in the toilet. That's it. That's the hierarchy of puke.

MOSCOW MULE

Can you guess what type of liquor is in a Moscow Mule? Here's a hint: it's vodka. Another old classic, the Moscow Mule is a vodka drink with a little bit of citrus to take the edge off. It's another simple drink that adds just a little splash of extra flavor to put it over the top and make you look like a genius. The brilliant part of these cocktails is that while knowing how to make them will make you seem impressive, there really isn't much to it at all.

**2 PARTS
GINGER BEER**

**1 PART
VODKA**

**1 SPLASH
LIME JUICE**

1. Add some ice to your cup, then pour together the ginger beer and vodka.
2. Top with a splash of lime juice and stir together. Enjoy.

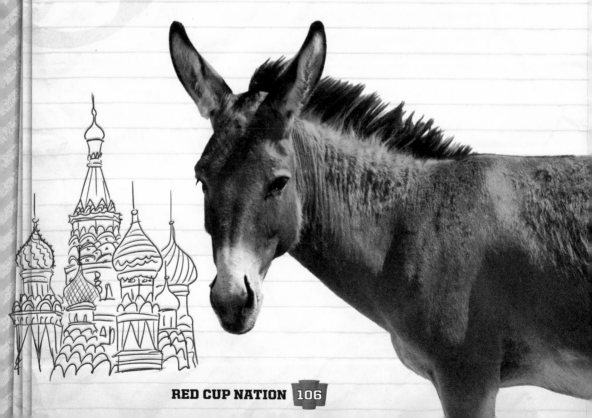

VARIATIONS

You can make just about any "Mule" you can think of. Try the Mexican Mule (made with tequila), the Cuban Mule (made with rum), the Irish Mule (made with whiskey)...you get the idea. It's so simple to make that swapping in your liquor of choice is always worth a try.

You know who loves weird and unusual drinkware like copper mugs? Hipsters. But that's okay! Drinking out of a copper mug doesn't automatically make you a hipster (well, okay, it kind of does, but you'll have to get past that). Kidding aside, having copper mugs and other cool drinkware on hand can add a little authenticity to your drinking, and make you feel like you're doing things right.

MINT JULEP

Okay, one more whiskey drink. Why not? When you want to look like you know your booze, whiskey should always be your go-to. There's a reason that liquor snobs always seem to be bourbon experts. You don't see people running around to "vodka tastings," do you? Well, maybe in Russia. But not in the Red Cup Nation! Anyway, the Mint Julep is the classic Kentucky Derby cocktail, so if you're hosting a get-together to watch the race, you can add an impressive display of authenticity to the event with a few of these babies. We'll get a little fancy here, because if you're serving Mint Juleps, you're probably not afraid to go the extra mile.

---

4 PARTS BOURBON WHISKEY

4 MINT LEAVES

1 MINT SPRIG (GARNISH)

1 PART WATER

1 DASH POWDERED SUGAR

1. Rip the mint leaves in half and toss them into your glass. Then add the sugar and water and mash them together a little. Don't use too much water—you really only need a little splash.

2. Fill the glass with ice, then add bourbon.

3. Stir everything together.

4. Garnish with a sprig of mint (trust me, this will make it look REAL nice) and enjoy.

VARIATIONS

Do you not have bourbon? Okay. Well, go ahead and use whatever whiskey you have, but just know that it's not going to be as good. And okay, I'll accept that you might not have powdered sugar. Regular sugar works. It's fine. I said it's FINE.

SORTA PIÑA COLADA

This is the last classy drink on the list. I've tried to stay away from giving you drinks that require a blender because, let's face it, a blender is a pain in the ass. But you might as well know how to make one frozen drink, because you never know when you're going to have a group to impress on a hot summer day. The Piña Colada is about as popular as any frozen drink out there, and has a really distinct flavor. I already told you to keep coconut rum around, and this is another great reason why.

---

1 PART WHITE RUM	1 PART COCONUT RUM	CRUSHED ICE (FOR BLENDING)
1 PART COCONUT MILK	2 PARTS PINEAPPLE JUICE	1 MARASCHINO CHERRY (GARNISH)

1. Put everything together in a blender and BLEND, baby.

2. Pour the resulting mixture into your cup and top it with a maraschino cherry (you did get maraschino cherries like I told you to, didn't you?). Enjoy.

VARIATIONS

For a little added flavor, you might consider including some triple sec or other liqueur. You can also omit the coconut rum if you want, but it really does add something to the drink.

SEE YOU ON THE OTHER SIDE!

HARD MODE

You know what goes down easy? Just about everything you've read so far in this book. But what good is drinking without a little challenge? Once in a while you just want to get together with a few friends and see who can come up with the most ridiculous boozy combination. Mixing shots with beer. Mixing different liquors. Adding hot sauces. Chili peppers. Gin and whiskey? You savage.

So forget easy mixers. Forget adding orange juice or Coke. No more cranberry juice, and no more ginger ale. In this section, we go hard. In this section, it's not about flavor. It's about downing a drink made from nothing but liquor and beer and pretending it didn't burn the whole way down. It's about watching your buddy's eyes water when he takes the shot you poured for him. Really, it's about pride.

So buckle up. There is absolutely no good reason to consume any of the drinks contained in this section, but, then again, that's kind of the point.

THE ENABLER

The Enabler is about spectacle. It's about creating a conversation piece that will sit in your living room and make every guest who wanders into your home say "wow, these people drink a lot." The first step is to find a water cooler. You know the type: holds a five-gallon jug, has "hot" and "cold" levers, people stand around it and talk about the game. Then it's the express train to flavortown with five gallons of whiskey and tea. Does it have to be whiskey and tea? No. But I strongly recommend you don't use anything carbonated. That will go flat IMMEDIATELY and leave you with five gallons of undrinkable sludge. Much better to make something that will keep, giving you a delicious, ice-cold drink whenever you want one.

---

2 PARTS
WHISKEY

3 PARTS
ICED TEA

1. Take a five gallon water jug and empty out the water.

2. Pour in a gallon of iced tea, then a gallon of whiskey, alternating until the jug is full. It is impossible to shake or stir a jug like this, so this is the best way to make sure the drink is sufficiently mixed.

3. Turn the jug over onto your water cooler, and presto! Ice cold whiskey and tea at your fingertips at all times.

How permissive is your office? Let's face it, this would make a pretty phenomenal addition to any office party. Forget boring old glasses of wine and the occasional under-chilled mid-range beer. Pop the top off the water cooler and go to town! I can all but guarantee that the quality of your office water cooler conversations have nowhere to go but up, so let's give everyone a helping hand.

FOUR CORNERS

Do you like rum? How about whiskey? And how do you feel about gin and vodka? If you're a seasoned drinker, you'll probably have any or all of them in a given night. But how about all at once? As in, in one shot glass? If that sounds good to you, you may not be right in the head. But if it sounds like a rite of passage that you'd like to put your friends through, then maybe this drink is exactly your speed. Featuring something from every corner of the liquor spectrum, this one is gonna burn.

1 PART **WHISKEY**	**1 PART** **VODKA**
1 PART **GIN**	**1 PART** **RUM**

1. Pour each liquor into a shot glass in equal parts.
2. Knock it back. I'd say "enjoy," but, well, you know.

Don't get confused: this drink may share a name with a childhood classroom game, but the target audiences are very different. Although, now that you mention it, it does seem like something that could easily be made into a drinking game. Play Four Corners, take a drink every time you lose. Look at that, we just invented a new drinking game! Good team effort, everybody.

THE ROCK

Speaking of things that will burn all the way down, we've come to The Rock. The Rock, maybe more than any other drink in this book, is an abomination. You should not drink it. You should not give it to anyone to drink. In fact, if you have any sense, you should probably just tear this page out of the book entirely before you get tempted to make something this vile. But if you like a challenge, and you're up for downing something that human taste buds do not have the ability to enjoy, The Rock is about as hardcore as it gets.

| ½ CAN MILWAUKEE'S BEST (OR OTHER SIMILARLY CHEAP BEER) | 1 SHOT WHISKEY | 1 SHOT RUM |

1. Crack open a can of Best and pour half of it into your cup.
2. Add a shot of whiskey and a shot of rum to the concoction. Drink up!

VARIATIONS

You can add whatever types of alcohol you want to this mixture. I can pretty much guarantee you that nothing is going to make this taste good, so go wild.

THE MINI MARY

If you want a Bloody Mary, skip to page 128. The Mini Mary answers the question of "what if you took a Bloody Mary and removed all of the things that make it taste good?" That's right, with the Mini Mary you're left with pretty much just vodka and hot sauce. But don't worry, we'll add a little extra flavor. How about some Worcestershire sauce? And pepper! Perfect! That's just about guaranteed to leave you gasping for air.

1 SHOT VODKA

5 DROPS HOT SAUCE

3 DROPS WORCESTERSHIRE SAUCE

1 PINCH PEPPER

1. Pour yourself a shot of vodka.

2. Add 5 drops of hot sauce and 3 drops of Worcestershire sauce.

3. Top with a tiny pinch of pepper and knock it back.

THE HEAT DEATH OF THE UNIVERSE

As long as we're incorporating hot sauce into drinks, let's try one that will REALLY light your mouth on fire. If you've never had chili whiskey before, you're probably doing yourself a favor. It's not the greatest tasting thing ever created. Sure, it has its uses—it's great in a Bloody Mary—but as a liquor to sip or do shots of, it's not ideal. Which DOES make it ideal for this section! Add a little hot sauce to that baby and let 'er rip. Just don't say I didn't warn you.

---

1 SHOT
CHILI OR PEPPER WHISKEY

5 DROPS
HOT SAUCE

1. Pour yourself a shot of chili (or pepper) whiskey.
2. Add in 5 or so drops of hot sauce and shoot it down!

The Heat Death of the Universe is, of course, not to be confused with the heat death of the EARTH, which will probably occur sometime just before the last Republican senator finally admits that, alright, MAYBE there's something to this whole "global warming" thing.

GLUE GUN

Here's a particularly gross one for you. Similar to the popular (and also disgusting) Cement Mixer shot, the Glue Gun mixes up the formula a bit: rather than mixing the ingredients together in your mouth, just take one shot after the other. This way, while you don't have to consume a disgusting glob of curdled Bailey's, you'll still have all the wonderful effects of effectively having your mouth glued shut by this disgusting one-two punch. You need to be prepared for this one—if you think curdled Bailey's is going to upset your stomach in any way, it's probably best to avoid it (frankly, it's probably best to avoid it anyway).

---

1 SHOT
LIME JUICE

1 SHOT
BAILEY'S IRISH CREAM

1. Pour a shot of lime juice and a shot of Bailey's.

2. Drink the shot of lime juice, then quickly follow it with the Bailey's.

3. Feel disgusted at yourself as your entire mouth is coated with a sticky, greasy, congealed mass of curdled Bailey's remnants.

FAST FORWARD

Do you often find that you can't get drunk quickly enough? Is your tolerance so high that you need some way to accelerate the process a little at the beginning of the night? That sounds like a bad idea, but if you're really dedicated to it, then you could definitely do worse than drinking a Fast Forward. It's got enough alcohol in it to do exactly what its name implies: fast forward you to a state of increased drunkenness that might otherwise take forever. And hey, it's better than sitting there ripping shots one after another, right? That sort of behavior is just concerning.

---

1 STOUT BEER

2 SHOTS
VANILLA VODKA

1. Pour a stout (or other dark beer) into your cup.
2. Add two shots of vanilla vodka. The vanilla flavor may come through, but chances are you won't even be able to tell there's any extra alcohol in the drink thanks to the overpowering flavor of most stouts.

CHEESY MARTINI

Martinis are always classy, right? WRONG! It turns out that there are plenty of ways to ruin even the most time-honored classics. You've probably heard of a Dirty Martini, served with an olive? Well, here's a thought: what if you served it with an olive...stuffed with bleu cheese? If that sounds absolutely disgusting, that's because it is! Nothing like a little bleu cheese floating in your drink—and there will be plenty of it, because you'll be adding it yourself.

**3 PARTS
GIN**

**1 PART
DRY VERMOUTH**

**1 BLEU CHEESE
STUFFED OLIVE**

**1 PINCH
CRUMBLED BLEU CHEESE**

1. In this case, I think it's pretty safe to say that you don't need a cocktail glass. Go ahead and add the gin and vermouth to whatever cup you want, and stir them together.

2. Add a bleu cheese stuffed olive and top with a little dusting of bleu cheese crumble. Enjoy (or not).

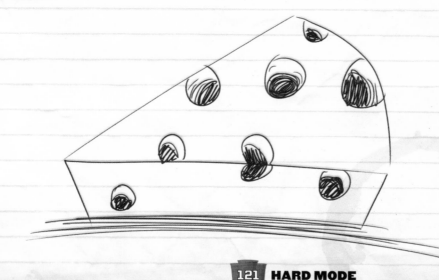

BBQ

ZZZ
ZZZ
ZZZZ
ZZZZZ
ZZZZ

THE WAKE-UP CHECKLIST

Okay, so you're awake. You were at a party the night before, but your memory is a little fuzzy. Chances are, you're wondering a few things. What happened? What should you do now? Why does everything hurt? And where is the nearest Taco Bell?

Before you head up the street for a breakfast sandwich, there are a few things you need to do to take stock of your situation. Fortunately, I'm here to help.

1. ESTABLISH LOCATION. This might seem pretty straightforward, but open your eyes and take a look around. Are you in your own home? If so, that's great! If not, where are you? Are you still at the party? (oh no!) Are you at a police station? (double oh no!) Are you lying in a field under a soccer net? (goal!) These are important things to know.

2. FIGURE OUT IF ANYONE IS WITH YOU. Is someone in bed with you? Do you know who they are? Are they in your house or are you in theirs? This is also important to know before you make a plan of action.

3. CHECK YOUR POCKETS. I'll note here that step 2.5 is "find your pants." Check your pockets. Look for receipts. 7/11 receipt for buying Gatorade? Congratulations! Looks like Drunk You knows how to take care of Sober You! 7/11 receipt for buying 14 taquitos? Oh no! Looks like Drunk You is an asshole and you'll be spending some quality time in the bathroom today!

4. CHECK YOUR TEXT MESSAGES. I know you don't want to. Believe me, I know. Reading the horrific and embarrassing things you sent while you were drunk is the worst thing a person can do. But you have to. Before you can start damage control, you need to know exactly who you horribly offended and how.

5. APOLOGIZE TO LITERALLY EVERYONE. Just kidding, it's probably not worth it. If you're reading this book, odds are good that "I was drunk" still flies as a valid excuse for you.

LIQUID STEAK

Maybe you've heard of shots called "liquid steak." The thing is, most of those shots are boring. A little Worcestershire sauce added to a shot of booze? What the hell is that? No, we can do better. There are plenty of other ways to make your shot steakier. How about some BBQ sauce? Salt? Pepper? Oh, and I know: let's finish it with a little dollop of mashed potato. Only a truly sick person would do a shot like this.

---

1 SHOT VODKA

3 DROPS WORCESTERSHIRE SAUCE

1 SQUEEZE BBQ SAUCE

1 PINCH SALT

1 PINCH PEPPER

1 SMALL DOLLOP MASHED POTATO

1. Pour a shot of vodka.
2. Add the Worcestershire sauce and BBQ sauce.
3. Top with a pinch of salt and pepper.
4. Finish with a little dollop of mashed potato and knock this sucker back. Godspeed.

BORDER LOVE

What could be more Mexican than tequila? And what could be more American than ranch dressing? With cultural and international harmony in mind, why not join the two together to create one beautiful drink? Well, it turns out that although each ingredient is delicious on its own, they combine about as well as peanut butter and motor oil. Still, if you're looking for a challenge...drink up!

---

1 SHOT
GOLD TEQUILA

1 SQUEEZE
RANCH DRESSING

1. Pour yourself a shot of tequila.
2. Add in a quick squirt of ranch dressing. Then knock it back, you sick, sick bastard.

VARIATIONS

Feeling really American? Crumble some Doritos and sprinkle them on top of the shot. Now we're cooking with gas!

THERE IS NO CURE
ONLY SUFFERING

PARTY ON WAYN

HANGOVER CURES

MORE BOOZE!

If you've consumed anything in this book so far, chances are you're going to be pretty hungover in the morning. Fortunately, there's an easy solution to every hangover, and it involves more of the hard stuff! I have no idea where the phrase "hair of the dog" comes from (sounds pretty gross, right?), but it's tough to deny that a little of last night's poison makes the morning a little bit easier.

There are classic hangover cures like the Bloody Mary and the Mimosa, but it's also possible to take cues from these drinks and concoct new ones that can be equally effective at taking a little of the edge off. And if there's one thing *Red Cup Nation* is all about, it's taking the edge off of life.

So if you wake up in the morning and your head is pounding, your eyes won't focus, and your stomach feels like it spent the night on a roller coaster, relax. Don't worry. These recipes will have you feeling shipshape (not really sure where that phrase came from, either) in no time.

BLOODY MARY

The queen of all hangover cures. Who doesn't love a good Bloody Mary? Actually, the answer is me, because I can't stand tomato juice. But hey, different strokes and all that. For those of you who DO love a good Bloody Mary (and you do seem to be the vast majority), here's how to go about making one that will more than satisfy you. And you know what the best thing about a Bloody Mary is? The garnishes. A good Bloody Mary won't just cure your thirst: it'll satisfy your hunger, too.

1 PART VODKA	1 SPLASH WORCESTERSHIRE SAUCE	1 PINCH SALT
2 PARTS TOMATO JUICE	1 SPLASH HOT SAUCE	1 CELERY STICK (GARNISH)
1 SPLASH OLIVE JUICE	1 PINCH HORSERADISH	1 RASHER OF COOKED BACON (GARNISH)
1 SPLASH LEMON JUICE	1 PINCH BLACK PEPPER	3 OLIVES (GARNISH)

1. Pop some ice into your cup and add the vodka and tomato juice. Stir 'em up.

2. Add in a splash of olive juice, a splash of lemon juice, a splash of Worcestershire sauce, and a few drops of hot sauce.

3. Now hit it with a little bit of horseradish, black pepper, and salt. Stir it up again!

4. Garnish with some bacon, celery, and olives, as well as anything else you want. Some places will garnish a Bloody Mary with an entire cheeseburger. If that speaks to you, I say go for it.

VARIATIONS

Did you hear me? I said you can customize this any way you want. Really, the only constants are the vodka and tomato juice. If the salt and pepper are too much for you, get rid of them. If you want to add some Old Bay seasoning, do it. The world is your oyster. Or Bloody Mary, as the case may be.

MIMOSA

It's hard to go wrong with a classic Mimosa. It's on every brunch menu known to man, but it's also one of the easiest drinks to make for yourself. Why go to a restaurant and pay $8 for half orange juice, half champagne? Just crack open a bottle and mix them for you and your friends all morning long from the comfort of your own home. Honestly, the markup on Mimosas is about as bad as it could possibly be. You can get a whole bottle of champagne for the same price! And then, hey, maybe you don't even need the orange juice. I won't tell.

---

1 PART CHAMPAGNE

1 PART ORANGE JUICE

1. Put some ice in your cup. Pour in the champagne.

2. Top with orange juice and stir it up. It's at this point that I feel I should point out that Mimosas are usually served in a wine glass or champagne flute, but I know you're not going to do that. Which is fine. You can fit, like, a quarter of a bottle in a standard red cup!

MMMM BREAKFAST BOOZE

RED WINE MIMOSA

Here's a little bud for your bowl: did you know Mimosas can be made with alcohol OTHER than champagne? It's true! The Red Wine Mimosa is a pretty great alternative to the tra-ditional orange juice and champagne Mimosa. This shouldn't come as a surprise—orange juice mixes surprisingly well with other juices, including grape and cranberry juice. Get your hands on some red wine and you can mix yourself a delicious new morning cocktail.

**1 PART
RED WINE**

**1 PART
ORANGE JUICE**

**1 SPLASH
CLUB SODA**

1. Add ice to your cup and combine the red wine and orange juice.

2. Top with a splash of club soda to give it a little fizz.

3. Stir together and enjoy!

VARIATIONS

If you've got sparkling red wine handy, you can skip the club soda. The club soda is only there to give the drink that extra bump of carbonation that you expect from a Mimosa, so if you can get that fizz another way, go for it.

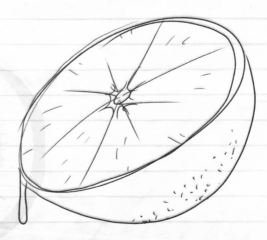

RED CUP SANGRIA

This is more of a large batch cocktail, but since it's usually a morning drink it seemed fitting to include it here. A little wine. A little juice. A little splash of liquor. With all the fresh fruit you can slice before your hangover gets the better of you. Everyone loves Sangria, and it's a pretty straightforward drink to make. The thing is, it usually has brandy or some other, similarly lame booze in it. I know you don't have that sitting around. Fortunately, this is Red Cup Nation, where the people are resourceful and there's always a workaround.

**4 PARTS
RED WINE**

**1 PART
GRAPE JUICE**

**WHATEVER FRUIT
YOU HAVE LYING
AROUND**

**1 PART
ORANGE VODKA**

**1 PART
CLUB SODA**

1. Slice up whatever fruit you have lying around. Apples, oranges, pineapples...whatever. This will all go into the drink once you've finished mixing it, so just keep that in mind.

2. Combine the wine, vodka, grape juice, and club soda and stir well.

3. Add the fruit and let it soak for a bit (overnight, if possible. This is a great drink to make while you're still sober, before things get too crazy).

4. Pour into cups and enjoy!

CELTIC COFFEE

Similar to the ever-popular Irish Coffee cocktail, Celtic Coffee kicks things up a notch while eliminating the fluff (read: whipped cream). Who needs all that sweetness when your head is killing you and you feel like you need sunglasses indoors? No, forget all that. Celtic Coffee is just coffee and booze, helping you wake up while taking the edge off your hangover the quick and easy way. Oh, and this probably goes without saying, but don't drink this out of a plastic cup. Seriously. You'll burn your hands. You can be hungover all you want, but try not to be THAT hungover.

**1 PART
JAMESON IRISH WHISKEY**

**1 PART
BAILEY'S IRISH CREAM**

**4 PARTS
HOT COFFEE**

**SUGAR
(OPTIONAL)**

1. Pour about a shot worth of Jameson into your mug and add coffee.

2. Top with a quick pour of Bailey's and stir everything together.

3. If you take your coffee with sugar, add it in and stir again. Enjoy!

CARIBBEAN COFFEE

How about something with a slightly more tropical bend? Alright, so I'd be hard pressed to call coffee tropical, but the Caribbean Coffee adds a nice coconut note to help nurse your hangover. This drink is a little less in-your-face than the Celtic Coffee—there's none of that whiskey harshness here. Instead, there's the cool, soft flavor of coconut rum to help ease you back into the land of the living. Once again, please don't use a literal red cup for this.

**1 PART
COCONUT RUM**

**1 PART
COCONUT MILK**

**4 PARTS
HOT COFFEE**

**SUGAR
(OPTIONAL)**

1. Pour the coconut rum and coffee together in a mug.
2. Top with a splash of coconut milk and stir thoroughly.
3. If you take your coffee with sugar, add it in and stir again. Enjoy!

MORNING SUNSHINE

There's an old adage that says "whiskey is sunlight held together by water." If that's true, then there's no reason you shouldn't mix yourself a whiskey drink as soon as the sun makes its way over the horizon, right? Sometimes the best way to cure your hangover is to get right back on that horse, and diving into a drink that's mostly whiskey is one way to do that. Don't worry, we'll add a little something to make it breakfasty.

**3 PARTS
BOURBON WHISKEY**

**1 PART
CLUB SODA**

**2 DROPS
BITTERS**

**1 PART
MAPLE SYRUP**

**1 PINCH
BROWN SUGAR**

1. Add the bourbon and maple syrup and stir them together as best you can. It's hard to get an ingredient as thick as maple syrup to cleanly combine, so if you DO have a cocktail shaker, now is the time to break it out.

2. Add a pinch of brown sugar and two drops of bitters. Stir again.

3. Top with a splash of club soda. You can either stir it in or leave it floating on top. Enjoy!

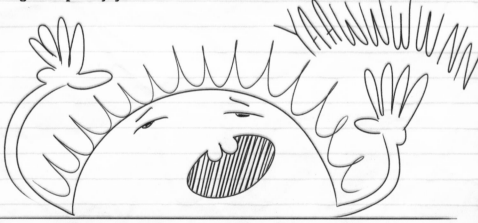

EARLY RISER

If you've ever had an Americano, you know it can be something of an acquired taste. So forget that. Instead, let's draw some inspiration from that old classic and mix up something fresh and original. The Early Riser is part Americano, part Vodka Sunrise, and 100% delicious. It's a great way to wake up and have a drink without feeling like you're jumping right back into the party mindset. It's easy to drink and easy to make.

**1 PART
VODKA**

**1 PART
SWEET VERMOUTH**

**3 PARTS
ORANGE JUICE**

**1 SPLASH
CLUB SODA**

1. Add ice to your cup, then add the vodka and orange juice together and stir.

2. Top off with the sweet vermouth and add a splash of club soda. It's up to you whether you want to stir these in or not. Enjoy!

ALL THESE GLASSES ARE EMPTY

THE BEST DAY TO DRINK

Which day of the week is the best day for drinking? Scholars and philosophers have debated the question for thousands of years. Which one offers the perfect combination of need, desire, and convenience?

Fortunately, unlike the great thinkers of the past (suck it, Hobbes), I have solved this dilemma. Let's look at the rundown:

MONDAY: The first day of the week for class, making it your first opportunity of the week to skip class. Is there anything more satisfying than starting the week off with a bang? And even if you do go to class, you'll need a beer afterwards. For these reasons, Monday is the best day of the week to drink.

TUESDAY: You're easing into the week. If you went to class Monday, you're DEFINITELY skipping Tuesday. You've earned it, after all. And with three more days in the week to look forward to, you can already tell it's going to be a SLOG. For these reasons, Tuesday is the best day of the week to drink.

WEDNESDAY: Hump day. Middle of the week. When could you possibly need a beer to get you through the day more than Wednesday? For these reasons, Wednesday is the best day of the week to drink.

THURSDAY: Thirsty Thursday is practically Friday. You didn't schedule any classes for Friday, did you? You did? Ouch. Well, you'll DEFINITELY need a drink on Thursday, then. Obviously Thursday is the best day of the week to drink.

FRIDAY: It's the weekend. Well, more or less. No classes on Saturday, that's for sure. And if you skipped class today, you'd have a three-day weekend. Maybe you should just text your buddies and see what they're up to. You know, just to see. If they're up for it, you can show them why Friday is the best day of the week to drink.

SATURDAY: I mean, college football is on. What, are you supposed to NOT drink during college football? Saturday is clearly the best day of the week to drink.

SUNDAY: And pro football! Really, weekends are just one big football and booze festival. And so what if you have class Monday...if you're too hungover, you can just skip. Sunday is the best day of the week to drink, by far.

Okay, I cheated. The answer is every day. Every day is the best day of the week to drink.

WAKEUP CIDER

Okay, ONE more whiskey cocktail, but only because it's so easy to drink. Apple cider is an excellent morning drink in the fall, and, as we've already established, whiskey and cider go GREAT together. In this case, we'll give it a little touch of that fizz that most morning cocktails enjoy. It wakes you up, it gets you going, and it does help to mask the harshness of the alcohol. What more can you ask for in the morning? A couple of these and your hangover will be a thing of the past.

**1 PART
WHISKEY**

**2 PARTS
APPLE CIDER**

**1 PART
SPARKLING CIDER**

1. Add ice to your cup, then mix in the whiskey and apple cider.

2. Top with a splash of sparkling cider and stir everything together. Enjoy!

BRIGHT AND EARLY

Some people think that a few slices of melon make for a delicious and filling breakfast. I don't happen to be one of them, but I can see how someone a little bit (okay, a lot) healthier than me might be drawn to such a thing. Melons taste good! Tough to deny that. And melon liqueurs taste just as good, if not better. There has been a distinct lack of melon present in this book so far, so let's close out this section with a brightly colored and delicious melon-based breakfast cocktail that'll knock your hangover back to the Stone Age.

**1 PART
MIDORI MELON
LIQUEUR**

**1 PART
PINEAPPLE JUICE**

**1 PART
CLUB SODA**

1. Add ice to your cup and mix everything together.
2. Stir until everything is thoroughly mixed and enjoy!

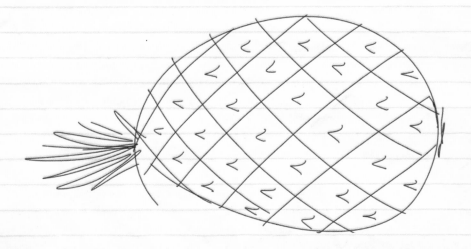

DRINKING GAMES

We all love alcohol, but sometimes you need a bump in the right direction to get the party started. After all, even the best-tasting cocktail in the world isn't much fun to drink if you're all just sitting around quietly. That's where drinking games come in.

Some drinking games require a lot of activity. For example, Dodgebeer is a game that should only be played outdoors, unless you don't mind your home being destroyed. On the other hand, all you need for a game of Kings is a deck of cards and a handful of beers. You can even center your drinking games around watching a movie or listening to a playlist of songs. They say "idle hands are the devil's playthings," and that definitely holds true when it comes to drinking games. No one is more inventive than a bored drinker.

So whether you're eager to embarrass your friends with a game of Truth or Dare or just looking to throw a ping-pong ball around, there's a drinking game for you. Browse this section for a nice mix of new games and classics...and a few new takes on some old favorites.

BUST OUT THE PING PONG BALLS!

BEER PONG
(AKA BEIRUT)

CLASSIC!

Number of Players: 2-4

WHAT YOU NEED

1 TABLE

20 CUPS

2-4 PING-PONG BALLS

4-8 BEERS

HOW TO PLAY

Whether you call it Beer Pong or Beirut, this is the classic drinking game to end all drinking games.

Divide into 2 teams and split up the cups so that each team has 10. Arrange the cups into a triangle at the end of the table (4 cups for the base, then 3, then 2, then 1). The triangle should be pointing at the other team. Now add beer to the cups (don't fill them completely, but add enough beer to keep the cups from jostling around—maybe ¼ full).

The goal is to throw the ping-pong balls into the other team's cups. Each team gets 2 shots per round, and when a ball lands in 1 of your cups, you must drink the beer in that cup and remove it from play. The first team to eliminate all of their opponent's cups wins.

RULES TO CONSIDER

- Each team gets 2 "re-racks." Twice, during the course of the game, each team can tell their opponents to rearrange the cups into a formation of their choosing.

- If both players make their shot on the same turn, they earn a "rollback." The other team must return the ping-pong balls and they each shoot again.

- If the ball bounces back toward the team that shot it and they are able to retrieve it before it touches the ground, they may shoot again—but the shot must be taken behind the back.

- Don't lean over the table. If your elbow crosses the edge of the table when you shoot, it is considered a penalty, and will cost you a cup.

ROCK PONG

(BEER PONG VARIANT)

Number of Players: 2-4

WHAT YOU NEED

1 TABLE	2-4 PING-PONG BALLS
20 CUPS	4-8 BEERS

HOW TO PLAY

Hard as a rock, Rock Pong is arguably the most difficult take on Beer Pong. Played just like regular Beer Pong, Rock Pong eliminates every frill. No re-racking cups. No rollbacks. No behind-the-back shots. This is a game of skill, and skill alone. The cups stay in exactly the same place at all times.

The one exception is this: when 1 team has hit every cup, the other team is permitted a "rebuttal," during which each player can shoot until they miss. During a rebuttal is the only time that re-racks are allowed, and the shooting team can request an unlimited number of "gentleman's racks," to put the cups in the position they prefer. If the team succeeds in hitting every cup during their rebuttal, the game enters a 3-cup overtime. The rules for overtime are the same as the rules for a regular Rock Pong game.

RULES TO CONSIDER

- The rebuttal and subsequent gentleman's racks are the only rules in Rock Pong. If you are wondering about any other rules that might give one team an advantage or extra shot—the answer is no.

QUARTER PONG
(BEER PONG VARIANT)

Number of Players: 2-4

WHAT YOU NEED

| 1 TABLE | 2-4 PING-PONG BALLS | 4-8 BEERS |
| 20 CUPS | 2 QUARTERS | |

HOW TO PLAY

Quarter Pong uses the exact same rules as Beer Pong, with one major difference: each team secretly places a quarter (or bottle cap or other signifier) in 1 of their cups. Neither team should know which cup their opponent's quarter is in, so each team should turn around when their opponent is placing their marker.

When the cup containing a team's quarter is hit, that team must do a shot of liquor. If 1 team wins the game and the other has not yet hit the cup with the quarter in it, the losing team must do an additional shot.

RULES TO CONSIDER

· If you're playing with 2 players per team, you can try playing with 2 quarters per side. Just be careful not to do too many shots too quickly.

MAGIC CUP
(BEER PONG VARIANT)

Number of Players: 2-4

WHAT YOU NEED

1 TABLE

22 CUPS

2-4 PING-PONG BALLS

4-8 BEERS

HOW TO PLAY

Magic Cup is played just like Beer Pong, with 1 major addition: 1 final cup placed anywhere in the room. Each team sets up 10 cups in classic Beer Pong formation. They then each take 1 more cup (the "Magic Cup"), and place it somewhere in the room. Whether it's on a bookshelf, behind a couch, on top of a television, or anywhere else, the cup can be placed wherever, just as long as the top is not covered and there is room to shoot a ping-pong ball into it.

Just like Beer Pong, the game is over when all of your opponent's cups have been hit. You can save the Magic Cup for last, you can go after it first, or you can have 1 person shoot at the formation and 1 person shoot at the Magic Cup each turn. It's up to you, but the game doesn't end until the Magic Cup has been eliminated.

RULES TO CONSIDER

- Since the Magic Cup can be hidden anywhere, you don't have to remain in your position behind the table to shoot at it. As long as you are at least 10 feet away from it, you can shoot from any place you choose.

- If you want, you can scrap the regular beer pong altogether and just play with 3-5 cups per team placed around the room.

FLIP CUP

Number of Players: 8

WHAT YOU NEED

---

1 TABLE   **8 CUPS**   **4-8 BEERS**

HOW TO PLAY

Flip Cup is a classic party game, and requires a long table and 8 cups. Divide 8 players into 2 teams of 4. The players stand side by side down the long side of the table, across from a player on the other team. Players have a plastic cup in front of them, filled however high you want as long as every cup has the same amount of beer.

When the game starts, the first pair of players must drink their beer as fast as they can, then attempt to flip their cup so that it lands upside-down on the table. You must place the cup on the edge of the table and flip it touching ONLY the bottom of the cup. You cannot touch the cup in the air or while it is landing—you can only touch the bottom of the cup on the initial flip, and keep trying until it lands upside-down.

Once the first player has successfully flipped his or her cup, the second player can drink their beer and begin the process again. This continues down the line until all four players have flipped their cups. The first team to finish wins.

RULES TO CONSIDER

· **Typically, the next player in line is not allowed to touch their cup until the previous player has successfully flipped theirs.**

DARTS

Number of Players: 2+

WHAT YOU NEED

1 TABLE

21 CUPS

3 PING-PONG BALLS

1-2 BEERS PER PLAYER

HOW TO PLAY

Darts is similar to beer pong, except all players shoot ping-pong balls from the same end of the table at one formation of cups.

Form the cups into a diamond shape: start with 1 cup in the center and arrange 8 cups in a diamond around it. When this is done, form the remaining 12 cups into another diamond around the outside. You should now have a diamond with 3 "rings." If it helps you visualize the rings, you might want to use different colored cups for the middle ring.

Each player gets 3 shots at the cups. A ping-pong ball in the outer layer is worth 1 point, a ball in the middle ring is worth 2 points, and a ball in the center cup is a bullseye, worth 3 points. The first player to reach 21 points wins the round. But beware—even numbers are not your friend. Drink twice for each 2-point cup you hit, and drink again if you end with an even score (for instance, a 3 point shot and a 1 point shot add up to 4).

RULES TO CONSIDER

- Like Beer Pong, keep your elbows behind the line or you'll cost yourself a drink.

- The game is to 21, but it must be 21 EXACTLY. If you go over, take one drink for every point over 21. Your turn is now over and you return to your original score before the turn.

DODGEBEER

Number of Players: 4

WHAT YOU NEED

AN OUTDOOR SPACE

1 TABLE

4 BEERS (IN CANS)

1 PING-PONG BALL

HOW TO PLAY

Dodgebeer is a game that requires a lot of room to move around (preferably on grass, to keep injuries to a minimum). Divide into 2 teams of 2 and stand at opposite ends of a table. Place 1 beer can upside down on each corner of the table. The beer on the corner closest to you is yours.

The goal is to finish your beer first. To play, each player takes turns throwing a ping-pong ball at the other team's beers. When the ball ricochets off the other team's beer, they must retrieve the ball and touch it to the table to end the turn. Until they touch the ball to the table, you can drink your beer. One throw per turn, alternating teams each turn.

The first time you hit their can, you might not have time to do much more than flip your beer over and get it open. That's okay—this is a game of inches. The first team to finish both of its beers wins.

RULES TO CONSIDER

· As always, don't lean over the table in an effort to give yourself an advantage.

· Don't throw too hard. If you knock over the other team's beer, any beer that spills will make it that much easier for them to finish first.

KINGS

Number of Players: 4+

WHAT YOU NEED

1 DECK OF CARDS   **1 CAN OF BEER**   **1-3 BEERS PER PLAYER**

HOW TO PLAY

The game is played as follows: place the beer can in the center of the floor or table and arrange the cards (facedown) in a circle around it. Try to arrange them as evenly as possible. Going around in a circle, each player must draw a card and perform the corresponding action. Kings has hundreds (thousands? MILLIONS?) of variants, and most people will add their own tweaks. This list will get you started:

2: You – The person who drew the card chooses someone else to drink.

3: Me – The person who drew the card drinks.

4: Floor – Everyone must touch the floor with one hand. Last person to do so drinks.

5: Guys – All guys playing the game must drink.

6: Chicks – All girls playing the game must drink.

7: Heaven – Everyone must reach for the ceiling with one hand. Last person to do so drinks.

8: Date – The person who drew the card picks a date. From now on, whenever one of you drinks, the other must drink.

9: Bust a Rhyme – The person who drew the card picks a word, and everyone around the circle must say a word that rhymes with it. First one to fail or repeat a word drinks.

10: Never Have I Ever – Everyone puts up 5 fingers and plays a quick round of Never Have I Ever. First to put all 5 fingers down drinks.

J: Categories – The person who drew the card chooses a category (ex: breakfast cereals, Pokémon, countries in Europe, etc.), and everyone around the circle must think of something within that category. First one to fail or repeat an answer drinks.

Q: Questions – Everyone around the circle may ask the person who drew the card one question. If they refuse to answer, they must drink.

K: Rule – The person who drew the card may create one new rule for the duration of the game.

A: Waterfall – Everyone must chug his or her drink. You may only stop drinking when the person to your right stops drinking. NOTE: only use this rule if everyone is drinking beer, not liquor.

RULES TO CONSIDER

- After each card is drawn, discard it by placing it under the tab of the beer can in the middle. When the seal breaks, the person who placed the last card must drink the beer. Until the beer is finished, they cannot talk.

- One alternate set of rules involves the "King's Cup." When each King is drawn, the person who drew it must pour some of their drink into a cup in the middle. The person who draws the final King must drink the resulting concoction.

NEVER HAVE I EVER

Number of Players: 4+

WHAT YOU NEED

NOTHING BUT DRINKS!

HOW TO PLAY

This game can be played using anywhere from 3-10 fingers, depending on how long you want each round to go. The gist of the game is this: when it's your turn, you say, "Never have I ever..." followed by something that you have never done, but you think the other players might have done. If they have, they must put a finger down and take a sip of their drink. If no one puts a finger down for your statement, you've struck out! Take a drink and try again.

The game is over when 1 player runs out of fingers. That player must finish their drink, and you can start again.

RULES TO CONSIDER

- If you want, you can institute a rule against "sniping," which is deliberately targeting one player with a highly specific statement. Of course, you could also decide that such gamesmanship is fair game.

DANGEROUS!!!

THIS ONE TOO!

TRUTH OR DARE

Number of Players: 4+

WHAT YOU NEED

NOTHING BUT DRINKS!

HOW TO PLAY

Truth or Dare! You probably haven't played Truth or Dare since high school! Maybe even middle school! But the truth is, it makes a surprisingly good drinking game now that you're older, bolder, and (let's face it), a little less inhibited.

The rules are simple. Arrange everyone in a circle. Whoever goes first can ask the person to their left, "Truth or Dare?" If they select truth, you may ask them any question. If they select dare, you may dare them to do something (as for what is considered reasonable, well, that depends on the group you're with!). If they refuse to answer the question or perform the dare, they must take a shot of liquor as punishment.

Once you have made it all the way around the circle, turn around and do it all again in reverse order. Not happy with the dare you received the first time around? Now's your chance for revenge.

Hopefully you aren't taking too many punishment shots, but this shouldn't be an all-night game. You don't want to do too many shots in a short period of time—that's a recipe for a bad night and a worse morning.

RULES TO CONSIDER

- You might want to include some way to overrule a dare if it's too outrageous. If more than half of the group thinks that the dare is out of line, then you should probably skip it. Of course, if you want to play hardball, more power to you.

SCREW THE DEALER

PLEASE!

Number of Players: 3+

WHAT YOU NEED

1 DECK OF CARDS

DRINKS FOR EVERYONE

HOW TO PLAY

One player holds the deck of cards, facedown. The player to the left guesses a card. The dealer looks at the top card, and says whether the card is either "higher" or "lower" than the guess. The player then guesses again. If the player guesses correctly, the dealer drinks. If the player guesses incorrectly, then the player must drink the difference between his final guess and the actual card (for instance, if the player's final guess is 7 and the card is a 3, the player owes 4 drinks). The next person in the circle now guesses a card, and so on.

When 3 people in a row have guessed wrong, the dealer passes the deck to the left. Now that person is the dealer until 3 people in a row guess wrong. As the game progresses and fewer and fewer cards are left, the odds of 3 wrong guesses in a row decrease, leaving the dealer feeling screwed—hence the name of the game.

RULES TO CONSIDER

- Arrange the discarded cards by value, to make it easier to see which cards have already been eliminated and make it even easier to screw the dealer.

MOVIE GAMES

Number of Players: 1+

WHAT YOU NEED

1 MOVIE YOU KNOW VERY WELL   **DRINKS FOR EVERYONE**

HOW TO PLAY

Once a movie hits some level of popularity, someone will almost certainly invent a drinking game for it. Many of these can be found online (just type "[movie title] drinking game" into Google and watch the results roll in), but you can also invent a new game if you know a movie particularly well.

For instance, you might drink anytime Darth Vader appears on-screen in *Star Wars*, or do a shot anytime Indy loses his hat in *Indiana Jones*. The possibilities are endless, and you can always add new rules as you go.

SONG GAMES

Number of Players: 1+

WHAT YOU NEED

1 SONG YOU KNOW VERY WELL

DRINKS FOR EVERYONE

HOW TO PLAY

As with movie drinking games, there are hundreds (if not thousands) of different drinking games geared towards popular songs. Pick a word or phrase from the song and take a drink every time it appears.

These games are great because they don't drag on—a typical song won't be more than three or four minutes long, so you can move onto the next one as quickly as you want. They're great games for pregaming before a night out, and a great excuse to get an extra beer or two in you before you head out the door.

One particularly popular song game is "Roxanne," and, as you might guess it involves taking a drink every time the word Roxanne appears in the Police song of the same name.

DRINK WHILE YOU THINK

(THE NAME GAME)

Number of Players: 4+

WHAT YOU NEED

NOTHING BUT DRINKS!

HOW TO PLAY

Drink While You Think is very simple—in fact, you can probably extrapolate how to play from the name alone. It's a classic game that's always fun to play in groups, and the booze will hit you hard if you're not careful!

Gather everyone together and arrange yourselves into a circle. The first person must say the name of a famous person, such as Tom Brady. The next person must say the name of a famous person whose first name begins with the same letter as the last name of the previous person (since Brady starts with B, they might say Burt Reynolds). Can't think of a name? That's too bad. Anytime you're thinking, you must also be drinking.

The game can conceivably go on forever, but you might want to stop playing if someone gives a name that has already been said, just to give yourselves an occasional break.

RULES TO CONSIDER

- If a player names someone whose first and last name both start with the same letter, some versions of the game call for play to be reversed.

- If a person finishes their drink in the middle of a turn, you can either make them get a new drink or simply move on to the next player in the circle.

- It's up to you whether you want to include the names of fictional characters, but it might make the game more interesting.

DRINK WHILE YOU THINK

(CATEGORIES)

Number of Players: 4+

WHAT YOU NEED

NOTHING BUT DRINKS!

HOW TO PLAY

A spin-off of Drink While You Think and Kings, this version of the classic drinking game expands beyond celebrity names and into just about anything you can think of. Remember the "Categories" rule in Kings? This is just like that—except instead of only drinking when you screw up, you drink the entire time you think.

Like Kings, the person who starts must name a category, such as "breakfast cereals." Going around the circle, each player must name a new breakfast cereal. Any time you spend thinking, you must also spend drinking.

When a player repeats something that has already been said, can't think of anything new, or otherwise fails to name something in the given category, the round is over. That person must drink, and the next person in the circle can choose a new category and begin a new round.

RULES TO CONSIDER

- You can institute a penalty for the player who ends the round. A typical penalty might be making them drink for 5 seconds.

WIN

SCOREBOARD

DO'S AND DON'TS

If you're looking to make friends at a party, there are a few things you should know. First off, most people are generally pretty friendly. If you've got things in common (which you probably do, since you're at the same party), it shouldn't be hard to strike up a conversation with anyone, guy or girl.

That said...there are still plenty of people who struggle with basic human interaction, who aren't quite sure when the appropriate time to interject into a conversation is. Here are some helpful do's and don'ts to get you started.

DO: Start a conversation with the person standing next to you watching the beer pong game.

DON'T: Start a conversation with someone playing in a beer pong game. They're concentrating, idiot.

DO: Approach an attractive partygoer and offer to get them another drink. That's a thoughtful conversation starter!

DON'T: Approach an attractive partygoer, hand them a drink, and say "drink this." That's a creepy way to get kicked out!

DO: Join a crowd of dancers and see if anyone cozies up to you. That's one way to make friends!

DON'T: Get handsy with strangers on the dance floor. That's another quick way to get kicked out. Or just flat-out kicked.

DO: Talk sports with someone wearing your favorite team's logo.

DON'T: Start trash talking someone wearing a rival team's logo. Everyone is drinking and tempers are likely to flare.

DO: Join the crowd helping someone perform a keg stand. Nothing builds bonds like camaraderie!

DON'T: Awkwardly ask strangers to help you do a keg stand. Come on, now.

SUPERLATIVES

Number of Players: 4+

WHAT YOU NEED

NOTHING BUT DRINKS!

HOW TO PLAY

Remember the superlatives in your high school yearbook? "Most Likely to Succeed." "Most Likely to be President." "Most Likely to be a Millionaire." On and on and on they go, each more uninteresting than the last.

This game is a lot like that, except a little more likely to go off the rails. "Most Likely to Succeed?" BORING. Forget the old standards and go with something on the risqué side. "Most Likely to Star in a Porno." "Most Likely to Throw Up at the End of the Night." "Most Likely to Wind Up in Jail." Pick any superlative you like, and the players must vote (you can't vote for yourself). Whoever gets the most votes must drink.

RULES TO CONSIDER

- Want to REALLY help the night along? If the decision is unanimous (aside from their own vote, of course), that person must take a shot of liquor.

SECRET SUPERLATIVES

Number of Players: 4+

WHAT YOU NEED

NOTHING BUT DRINKS!

HOW TO PLAY

A derivative of Superlatives, Secret Superlatives is a much sneakier game. You can learn a lot about what your friends think of you...but it'll cost you.

In Secret Superlatives, the game goes around the circle, with each person again thinking of a superlative, such as "Most Attractive Person in the Room," "Least Likely to Get Laid Tonight," and so on; however, in this game, you don't announce the superlative to the room. Instead, you whisper the superlative to the person on your left, and they must announce their answer to the room.

Did they say your name? Doesn't that make you wonder what the superlative was? What is it that they thought fit you perfectly? You can find out... but you'll have to do a shot.

It's a game where you want to pick your spots. Obviously you don't want to do a shot every time your name comes up—so the game is as much about reading people as anything else. Did they give you a weird look before saying your name? Are they refusing to make eye contact? Maybe this is where you pay the iron price and knock one back.

RULES TO CONSIDER

- Taking a shot is a steep price, but it ensures that you can't simply demand to know every superlative (after all, if you want to play that way you should just play the regular version of the game). That said, if you're concerned about players taking too many shots, you can always revert the price to simply taking a regular drink instead.

CHEERS, GOVERNOR

Number of Players: 4+

WHAT YOU NEED

NOTHING BUT DRINKS!

HOW TO PLAY

Cheers, Governor is a counting game, the goal of which is to count to 21. The game goes around the circle of players, each saying 1 number. When the count reaches 21, that person must say "Cheers, Governor!" They must then make a new rule corresponding to another number in the count.

Examples of rules might be "#8 must take a drink," "#15 must spin in a circle," or "#20 must kiss X player on the cheek." From then on, whoever says that number must adhere to the rule. Forget a rule or screw up your turn? Take a drink, and the count goes back to the beginning.

The game ends when there is a rule for every number and the count successfully makes it to 21 with no errors.

POWER HOUR

Number of Players: 1+

WHAT YOU NEED

DRINKS FOR EVERYONE   **1 CLOCK**

HOW TO PLAY

Some might argue that a Power Hour isn't technically a drinking game, but others would say it's as much a drinking game as any movie or song drinking game. At their core, drinking games are more about the social element than anything else, and in that regard a Power Hour can be an incredibly fun experience to share with friends.

The rules are simple: for 1 hour, you must take a shot of beer every minute. A shot of beer might not sound like much, but when you're doing 1 every minute, you'll feel the buzz sooner than you think.

Plenty of Power Hour mixes exist on YouTube or other internet sources, usually containing 60 one-minute songs. While it isn't necessary to use a playlist, it can be a good way to keep track of when it's time to drink again. If nothing else, it's a lot more fun than watching the clock.

WIZARD STAFF

Number of Players: 1+

WHAT YOU NEED

1 ROLL OF DUCT TAPE   **INFINITE BEERS**

HOW TO PLAY

Wizard Staff isn't a game so much as a competition: throughout the night, you must stack your finished beers on top of one another and duct tape them together. As the stack grows larger, it begins to resemble a staff—hence the name of the game.

Once your staff is taller than you are, you have officially earned the title "Wizard." Whoever has the tallest staff at the end of the night is the Wizard King, Chief Wizard, or whatever other honorary title you choose (the most common variation is "Wisest Wizard," which is lame, and you shouldn't use it).

RULES TO CONSIDER

- This should go without saying, but be mindful of your beer intake. Anytime you're playing a game where consumption is a competition, make sure you're using light beer with a relatively low ABV.

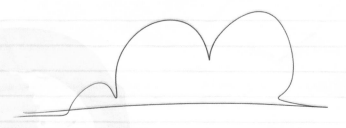

TERMINOLOGY

BOURBON WHISKEY: A type of whiskey mainly from the southern US. In technical terms, it's distilled from a mash of at least 51% corn and aged in charred oak barrels.

COCKTAIL SHAKER: A sealed container used to mix cocktails by shaking. Every bar has one, but most college students probably won't.

DASH: A quick addition, usually of a liquid ingredient. Equal to approximately 1 teaspoon, but not an exact measurement.

DOLLOP: A large spoonful.

LIQUEUR: A sweet, flavored type of alcohol. These tend to be pretty strong, and you wouldn't want to drink too many of them on their own.

PART: Measuring ingredients in "parts" allows you to scale the drink up or down as you please. If a drink is 1 part whiskey and 2 parts iced tea, you might add 2 oz. of whiskey (1 part) and 4 oz. of iced tea (2 parts).

SCOTCH WHISKEY: A specific type of whiskey from Scotland, aged in oak casks for at least three years. It tends to have a pretty smoky flavor.

SLICE OF FRUIT: A common garnish. Refers to a slice taken from a fruit circle.

SPLASH: A quick addition, usually of a liquid ingredient. Larger than a dash, equal to approximately a tablespoon, but not an exact measurement.